Preaching the Parables

I love parables! *Preaching the Parables: A Practical Model* has shown me how to go deeper in my personal study and preaching of Jesus's parables. I appreciate the insights we can gain from the "Picture-Mirror-Window-Door" model described here so clearly. The numerous illustrations of the process help the reader see how parables can come alive in diverse ways. The four authors, from New Zealand and Latin America, show the relevance of Jesus's beautiful parables across time and cultures.

Rev. Lynne Baab, PhD
Adjunct Associate Professor of Ministry and Biblical Studies,
Hope International University, California, USA

Picture, Mirror, Window, Door? How do Jesus's parables function? Do they provide information about reality, access to God, conviction about ourselves, insight into others, or all of the above? Is there a sequence in which we should expect these experiences to occur and are they identical in all parables? Paul Windsor has assembled an international, multicultural team of preachers to reflect on a good cross-section of Jesus's most famous stories with a view to answering these questions and doing some significant spadework to help those who would preach on these stories in whatever context they find themselves. Easy to read and understand, this book should bless many preachers – and other readers – around the world.

Craig L. Blomberg, PhD
Emeritus Professor of New Testament,
Denver Seminary, Colorado, USA

The parables of Jesus continue to inspire and challenge Christians, but they are not always easy to understand. *Preaching the Parables* is a treasure trove of wisdom and practical advice for the disciple and preacher. Written by pastors and teachers from across the world, this will become a valuable resource for the church today.

Sarah Harris, PhD
Research Fellow, Carey Baptist College, New Zealand

This book is a remarkable addition to the resources for preachers and teachers to understand the genre of parables with a simple and innovative approach. I highly commend the contributors for writing this invaluable resource with profundity and simplicity, especially keeping the oral-preference settings in mind. It is a must-read for anyone who wants to understand the parables of Jesus in an engaging and thorough manner.

Qaiser Julius, PhD
Director,
Open Theological Seminary, Lahore, Pakistan

How fit are the confines of traditional exegetical approaches for understanding and preaching Jesus's parables in the Scriptures? There is certainly value in such approaches, but these vivid and imaginative texts need a more creative framework, a breathing space!

Written by authors with experience in diverse backgrounds, *Preaching the Parables: A Practical Model* responds to this task by offering its readers a powerful combination. On the one hand, the authors present a model and a concrete set of elements through which a parable may be properly interpreted. On the other hand, there are plenty of small illustrations for different understandings of details in such texts, as well as a concrete set of examples of what a sermon on some of them would look like.

The end result is a solid structure where there is enough room for each reader, under the inspiration of the Holy Spirit, to work with their creativity and contextual approach for preaching the parables.

César Lopes, PhD
President,
Comunidad de Estudios Teologicos Interdisciplinarios (CETI), San José, Costa Rica

Books are good company, some, in a very special way, become travel companions, an always desired presence. *Preaching the Parables* is that type of work, one which we must always have at hand. Clearly and confidently, this book helps us study and preach the parables, without compromising the depth and beauty of their teaching. What a joy to have a book like this!

Ziel J. O. Machado
Honorary President, International Fellowship of Evangelical Students
Vice-Rector and Professor of Pastoral Theology,
Seminário Teológico Servo de Cristo, São Paulo, Brazil

This book is an inspiring handbook for preaching the parables. The Picture, Mirror, Window, Door model is presented simply and compellingly yet leaves room for a preacher's creativity. The book is also a model for intercultural humility and awareness, illustrating that a hearer's culture influences aspects of interpretation and therefore each culture can uniquely contribute to improving the global church's appreciation of how the parables work to inform, involve, shock, and shape us.

Ian W. Payne
Executive Director,
Theologians Without Borders

Finally, a book written from the perspective of evangelical theology that not only presents the most useful tools for interpreting the Master's parables, but also offers pastoral guidelines for preaching them in our churches! I began my task of preaching in the early 1980s and became enthusiastic about preaching parables, believing that they were ideal texts for a novice preacher from the neighborhood. However, even after all these years, I can confirm that they are profound texts for the interpreter and unfathomable for the soul.

This book skillfully guides us along the paths of parables, without avoiding their complexity. It teaches how to approach them, indicates the intricacies of their exegesis, and provides guidelines for getting treasures out of them, offering a practical guide to impart them from our pulpits.

How much it would have benefited me to have had a book like this in my first years of pastoral ministry. However, it comes at a good time, especially in this post-pandemic period, when the confusion has increased, the anxieties have multiplied, but the need for hope that the gospel offers us has also grown. I commend this to the reader and offer my sincere gratitude to the authors.

Harold Segura
Director of Faith and Development,
World Vision, Latin American and the Caribbean

Despite their familiarity, the parables of Jesus continue to puzzle, challenge, and intrigue their readers, hearers and – not least – their preachers. The co-operative work from different cultural backgrounds which has led to this accessible book on preaching the parables is therefore to be warmly welcomed. It offers a suggestive model for creative preaching based on the parables' dynamic rhetorical functions, together with helpful sample sermons. This model does not predetermine how any particular parable is to be interpreted, or preached on a particular occasion, but provides a framework within which preachers can seek to let the parables work their subversive magic on contemporary hearers in fresh ways. I trust it will be an inspiration to many across the world.

Stephen I. Wright, PhD
Formerly Vice Principal and Academic Director,
Spurgeon's College, UK

The charm and art of parables lies in communicating profound theology with great simplicity. This book helps to follow this path in preaching too: the fourfold structure of the approach (picture, mirror, window, door) is easy to remember, but it is broad enough to bring out the complexity of the texts. Above all, it aims – like the parables – to address the readers or listeners directly and invite them to be transformed in their faith, and see the others "beyond the Door."

Ruben Zimmermann, PhD
Professor of New Testament Studies,
Johannes Gutenberg University of Mainz, Germany
Author of *Puzzling the Parables of Jesus* (Fortress Press, 2015)

Preaching the Parables

A Practical Model

Geoff New and Wilfredo Weigandt
with
Paul Windsor and Esteban Améstegui

© 2025 Wilfredo Weigandt, Esteban Améstegui, Paul Windsor, and Geoff New

Published 2025 by Langham Preaching Resources
An imprint of Langham Publishing
www.langhampublishing.org

Langham Publishing and its imprints are a ministry of Langham Partnership

Langham Partnership
PO Box 296, Carlisle, Cumbria, CA3 9WZ, UK
www.langham.org

ISBNs:
978-1-83973-833-3 Print
978-1-83973-974-3 ePub
978-1-83973-975-0 PDF

Wilfredo Weigandt, Esteban Améstegui, Paul Windsor, and Geoff New have asserted their right under the Copyright, Designs and Patents Act, 1988 to be identified as the Authors of this work.

All rights reserved. No part of this publication may be reproduced, stored in a retrieval system or transmitted, in any form or by any means, electronic, mechanical, photocopying, recording or otherwise, without the prior written permission of the publisher or the Copyright Licensing Agency.

Requests to reuse content from Langham Publishing are processed through PLSclear. Please visit www.plsclear.com to complete your request.

Scriptures taken from the Holy Bible, New International Version®, NIV®. Copyright © 1973, 1978, 1984, 2011 by Biblica, Inc.™ Used by permission of Zondervan.

British Library Cataloguing-in-Publication Data
A catalogue record for this book is available from the British Library

ISBN: 978-1-83973-833-3

Cover & Book Design: projectluz.com
Illustrations: Jun Huang (Auckland, New Zealand) and the illustration on page 7, Natalia De la Fuente (Cochabamba, Bolivia)

Langham Partnership actively supports theological dialogue and an author's right to publish but does not necessarily endorse the views and opinions set forth here or in works referenced within this publication, nor can we guarantee technical and grammatical correctness. Langham Partnership does not accept any responsibility or liability to persons or property as a consequence of the reading, use or interpretation of its published content.

Contents

Foreword xi

1 The Story of Parable Interpretation 1
    Paul Windsor

2 The Skills for Interpreting the Parables 9
    Wilfredo Weigandt and Geoff New

3 Picture-Mirror-Window-Door 25
    Geoff New

Part 1

4 Look *at* the Picture 31
    Geoff New

5 Look *in* the Mirror 39
    Geoff New

6 Look *through* the Window 47
    Geoff New

7 Look *Beyond* the Door 57
    Geoff New

Part 2

8 The Parable of Three Men and a Lamb (2 Samuel 12:1–13) 67
    Paul Windsor

9 The Workers in the Vineyard (Matthew 20:1–16) 75
    Geoff New

10 The Tenants (Matthew 21:33–46) 85
    Wilfredo Weigandt

11 The Friend at Midnight (Luke 11:5–13) 95
    Geoff New

12 The Rich Fool (Luke 12:13–21) 103
    Geoff New

13	The Lost Coin (Luke 15:8–10) 113
	Esteban Améstegui
14	The Persistent Widow (Luke 18:1–8)......................... 119
	Wilfredo Weigandt
15	The Pharisee and the Tax Collector (Luke 18:9–14) 127
	Wilfredo Weigandt
	Epilogue... 135
	Wilfredo Weigandt
	Bibliography 137

Foreword

More than thirty years ago, Thomas Long observed that "preaching a parable is a novice preacher's dream, but often an experienced preacher's nightmare."[1] These simple little stories attract new preachers because they seem so easy and straightforward. However, as preachers linger with the parables, going deeper in their study of them, they realize that there is much more happening than they had seen in that first encounter.

The situation is complicated further by the fact that there has been more written about parables than about any other genre in the Bible. Clearly, understanding parables is not as straightforward as it may seem. Even experienced preachers easily become confused by the clutter of scholarship, fearful of getting things wrong. And not all that has been written is helpful. Klyne Snodgrass, writer of the most comprehensive evangelical book on the parables, contends that "the parables are the most abused literature ever."[2]

Nightmare and abuse. These are not pleasant words, especially when referring to the genre which is at the heart of the teaching ministry of Jesus. And yet, I can raise my hand as one who has tasted these experiences. Armed with my Kenneth Bailey book,[3] discovered at seminary, I commenced my pastoral ministry with a sermon series through the parables of Luke. I journeyed deeper into the academic discussion, with the history of the interpretation of the parables forming the basis of my dissertation, and the struggle to interpret parables correctly froze me as a preacher; I lacked confidence to preach the parables. But apart from the parable of the soils, only recently have I returned to the parables as a preacher.

This situation, whether it be for me or for others, is unacceptable.

There must be another way – and there is. It was at a Langham Preaching seminar in Hyderabad (India) in 2019 that things changed for me. Geoff New, who was teaching a session on preaching the parables, used this familiar model, first suggested by Warren Wiersbe, with Geoff extending Wiersbe's model: the parable starts as a picture, becomes a mirror, and then a window, before providing the listener with a door. I took this model and began experimenting

---

1. Long, *Preaching and the Literary Forms*, 87.
2. Snodgrass, *Stories with Intent*, 597.
3. Bailey, *Poet and Peasant*, and *Through Peasant Eyes*.

with it myself, especially during my years as a trainer in the indigenous, grassroots preaching movement in Pakistan.

The model seemed to work. People grasped what was happening as they moved through these stages. It was easy to remember, and it appealed to those whose preferred style is oral learning. I began to wonder about the possibility of a book, primarily as a resource for our Langham Preaching family.

At about this time, another strand in the story began to take shape. During the early months of the COVID-19 pandemic, there emerged a collection of poems – or laments – by Wilfredo Weigandt of Argentina. So moved were we by his poetry that we decided to publish these poems in a booklet to help sustain people, offering them words with which to express their words with which to voice their fears and frustrations during that dreadful time.[4] The book travelled across time zones, bringing comfort and strength to many. Trained as both an architect and a poet, Wilfredo is also a preacher who has been blessed with a capacity to engage with sermon-making as both a science and an art. Evidently, the contemplative tradition has shaped him, as it has done Geoff, giving them both a deeper insight into the text of Scripture.

Was it possible to draw these two people, unknown to each other and unable to speak a common language, into a collaborative effort to produce a book on preaching the parables? To do so, we needed to find one more person, someone who could help bridge the gap between English and Spanish. Esteban Améstegui of Bolivia – who combined a facility in both languages with expertise in media and communication, as well as learner-centred adult education – was the perfect solution.

Now it remained only to ask each of these people if they would like to participate in this project. They agreed. And so it came to pass that we met online regularly over a twelve-month period, with Geoff as our facilitator. The book gradually took shape. Chapter 1 tells the *story* of parable interpretation, while the *skills* for parable interpretation are described in chapter 2. The preaching model is introduced across chapters 3 to 7 and then utilized in chapters 8 to 15 to create sermons on eight parables, with contributions from each of us. Along the way, this journey was enhanced by advice about sketches from our friend Fred Brunell, the artist-priest. The final sketches were created by Jun Huang, Fred's friend from Auckland, New Zealand. The illustrated timeline at the end of chapter 1 was drawn by Esteban's friend, Natalia De la Fuente from Cochabamba, Bolivia.

---

4. Wilfredo Weigandt, *Prayer in the Time of a Pandemic*.

Of all the many pages written on the parables, some of my favourites are found in the opening and closing chapters of a book authored by Paul Simpson Duke.[5] On his very first page, he imagines the Bible to be like a house in which the rooms represent the different genres, with one of these rooms being "uniquely curious, beguiling, strange."[6]

On behalf of Esteban, Wilfredo, and Geoff, I invite you to enter that room with us.

Paul Windsor

---

5. Duke, *The Parables: A Preaching Commentary*.
6. Duke, 1.

1

The Story of Parable Interpretation

Paul Windsor

The story of parable interpretation begins in Sunday schools across history. The parable is an earthly story with a heavenly meaning. Didn't we all start with this description? A comparison is being made in the parable. Something earthly is stated while something heavenly is meant. There takes place a "transfer from the real world to the religious world."[1]

1854: The Allegory

The description of a parable as a story where a heavenly meaning is embedded in an earthly story has been traced to the Dutch scholar C. E. Van Koestveld,[2] writing in 1854. In modern times, we have become familiar with this description, especially following the popularity of writing such as C. S. Lewis's *Chronicles of Narnia*, which is recognized in English literature as allegory. However, this practice of embedding meaning is ancient. In the Hebrew Old Testament, the parable belongs to a type of writing (*mashal*) that is characterized by making comparisons. A few centuries later, in his discussion of the parable of the good Samaritan, the African church father Augustine took this approach to an extreme by attempting to demonstrate that *every* single detail in a parable has another meaning.

Often referred to as allegorizing, Augustine's approach persisted for centuries. However, at the dawn of the twentieth century, the German scholar

---

1. Snodgrass, *Stories with Intent*, 571.
2. As quoted in Tucker, *Example Stories*, 50.

Adolf Jülicher – opposing Augustine's view – argued that there was only one point of comparison in a parable and that the heavenly meaning is the only meaning to be drawn from the parable. This understanding endured; and even as late as the 1970s, it was suggested that the details in the parable simply "serve the main thrust of the parable, like the feathers which wing the arrow to its mark."[3]

1935: The Meal and the Optical Illusion

Over time, other features of this story of interpretation began to emerge. In 1935, the English scholar C. H. Dodd's description of the parable prepared the way for the developments in the story through the rest of the century:

> At its simplest the parable is a metaphor or simile drawn from nature or common life, arresting the hearer by its vividness or strangeness, and leaving the mind in sufficient doubt about its precise meaning to tease it into active thought.[4]

Dodd reaffirmed the earthly or realistic – "drawn from nature or common life" – feature in the parable. This recognition of the realism in parables surfaced in different ways throughout the developing story. Forty years after Dodd, Kenneth Bailey – having lived for some decades in the Middle East – argued that the realism came from the peasant culture in which Jesus lived. Bailey reminds readers that "as soon as the cultural base of the church ceased to be Middle Eastern/peasant, the parable inevitably became stories about foreigners."[5] And so, listening to the parables today is similar to sitting down to a meal with a family not our own, listening to their laughter as they reminisce – and feeling like an outsider. Sixty years after Dodd, William R. Herzog, writing as a social scientist, notes that "the parables were not earthly stories with heavenly meaning, but *earthy* stories with *heavy* meanings, weighted down by an awareness of the workings of exploitation in the world of their hearers."[6]

Dodd also observes that this realism has planted within it something exaggerated or unusual – "its vividness or strangeness" – which works to engage the listener – "tease ... into active thought." This is akin to an optical illusion where we look once and must then look again to be sure about what

---

3. Hunter, *Parables*, 12.
4. Dodd, *Parables of the Kingdom*, 16.
5. Bailey, *Poet and Peasant*, 27.
6. Herzog, *Subversive Speech*, 3.

we see – except that the parable is for the ear, not the eye. We *listen* once, and then we must listen again: "Did I hear that correctly? Can I hear it again?" This is because the parable often contains "a surprising, odd turn which shatters the realism, the everydayness of the story (and) evokes an unbelieving gasp."[7] There is a twist in the story, there is a paradox to be felt.

1954: The Political Cartoon

Returning to the chronology of the story of intrepretation, Joachim Jeremias, writing in 1954, reminds us that parables were "uttered in an actual situation of the life of Jesus . . . [as] weapons of controversy."[8] They are "stories with intent" – to borrow Klyne Snodgrass's book title – the intent of Jesus.[9] Therefore, to be accurately understood, parables must remain tied to the ministry of Jesus and his message of the kingdom of God, with that message carrying all the excitement of "pictures of revolution."[10] Here, the parables bear some resemblance to the political cartoon. Such a cartoon, which uses symbols that mingle the realistic with the exaggerated to provoke debate, only makes sense within a specific situation. You will probably be able to think of occasions when a political cartoon resulted in a shocked outcry by sections of a community or nation. Such times of controversy capture something of the impact of Jesus's parables within his Jewish world.[11]

While on the subject of the "actual situation" of the parable, another point to remember is that the parables were "used twice – once by Jesus and then again by the Evangelists."[12] As we do with the Epistles, we acknowledge that the evangelists – the writers of the Gospels – were working through their own agenda under the inspiration of the Spirit. While they did different things with the parables of Jesus – placing them here or there, adding this introduction and that conclusion – they were guided by the same Spirit.

---

7. Donahue, *Gospel in Parable*, 75.
8. Jeremias, *Parables of Jesus*, 21.
9. Snodgrass, *Stories with Intent*.
10. The phrase "pictures of revolution" is the subtitle of Wenham's book, *Parables of Jesus*.
11. See Klausen, *Cartoons*.
12. Snodgrass, *Stories with Intent*, 26.

1964: The Painting

The next stage in the story of parable interpretation recognized that the parable is a work of art. While this feature was anticipated by Dodd,[13] it was only in 1964, in the work of G. V. Jones, that this approach came into focus. Jones, who viewed the parables as forms of narrative art, notes that "the work of art is independent of time."[14] Jesus was an artist, not just a teacher. Here, the parable is seen as complete within itself. It does *not* need to be tied to a historical occasion, or even a literary context, to be meaning-full.

The parable is like a painting that conveys meaning regardless of the location of the art gallery in which it is placed. Viewers are drawn into the painting – or the parable – seeing whatever they wish to see in it because its meaning is open-ended. "If a picture can express a thousand words, then a parable can express a thousand expositions."[15] This quotation captures something of what Henri Nouwen communicates in his discussion of Rembrandt's *The Return of the Prodigal Son*, which is a parable expressed as a painting. Nouwen demonstrates how it might be the father, the elder brother, or the prodigal son in the painting who captures the viewer's attention; and he comments that this experience is not one that can be adequately expressed in words.[16]

We are beginning to feel some tension in this story, aren't we? The earlier approaches are more historical, focusing on the situation and intention of the author. These newer approaches are more literary in the way their focus remains within the text or on the parable itself as the way to uncover meaning.

1974: The Joke

As the story of interpretation continues, so does the tension because it is not just the author *behind* the parable and the text *within* the parable that shape interpretation but, now, the listener *in front of* the parable must also be taken seriously.

---

13. "The parables have an imaginative and poetical quality. They are works of art, and any serious work of art has significance beyond its original occasion." Dodd, *Parables of the Kingdom*, 146.

14. Jones, *Art and Truth*, 123.

15. Young, *Jewish Parables*, 4.

16. See Nouwen, *Return of the Prodigal*. See also Scott, *Hear Then*, 419: "Each parable is a gem. At whatever angle you hold it to the light, the gem and the light will appear pristinely different, as though never before seen. The parables are always refracted anew in the angle of each new performance."

It helps to start with some examples. Take the parable of the good Samaritan (Luke 10:25–37) and the parable of the Pharisee and the tax collector (Luke 18:9–14). Listeners are conditioned to identify with the hero in a story. So, when *today's* listeners enter these stories, they identify with the Samaritan and the tax collector, feeling aligned with the good lives of these heroes. And yet, when *Jesus's* listeners entered these stories, the message is subverted because in each story their hero, with whom they had identified turns out to be the villain. Over time, the impact of these parables has been reversed because of this change in the listeners.

This next stage in the story of interpretation takes the listener seriously. In 1974, the American scholar J. Dominic Crossan expressed the idea that "a parable is a story whose surface structure allows its deep structure to invade one's hearing in direct contradiction to one's expectation."[17] This is similar to what happens with a joke such as a Mr. Bean comedy sketch. A joke has a "surface structure" that develops in line with the familiar and the real, progressing according to "one's expectation." The listener is nodding in agreement, even knowing what is coming next. With each step, the anticipation builds towards the punchline. In Crossan's words, this punchline is that moment of "invasion," which operates in "direct contradiction" to what is expected. "Parables often contain elements of reversal"[18] by which the thinking and behaviour of listeners is changed. The Samaritan turns out to be the neighbour, the tax collector is praised.

2015: The Trampoline

The twenty-first century brought a new impulse into the story of parable interpretation: integration or combining the different interpretations. After almost two hundred pages devoted to surveying the story, just a few paragraphs from the end of his discussion, Craig Blomberg writes, "Almost every method has made important contributions, and a full-orbed exegesis will do its best to adopt an eclectic approach."[19] Three years later, in 2015, Ruben Zimmermann introduced his own "integrative method" with these words:

> My own goal is to seek a "binding openness" which, on the one hand, accepts a great variety of interpretations but on the other

---

17. Crossan, "The Good Samaritan," 98.
18. Snodgrass, *Stories with Intent*, 19.
19. Blomberg, *Interpreting the Parables*, 189.

hand does not relinquish an overarching intepretative framework for the truth of the parables.[20]

Further on in his book, he comments that

> the approach of this volume is marked by the conviction that historical author, text and recipient all belong together and that meaning is constituted in and through their reciprocal engagement with each other.[21]

One way to capture this "binding openness" or "reciprocal engagement" is with the image of a trampoline – the kind used by gymnasts. This trampoline has a frame with a mat that is connected to three sides by multiple springs. The frame represents the need "to keep people in the context of Jesus."[22] The mat represents the parable, freed to bounce – that is, to create meaning for us – by acknowledging the multiple springs on each of its three sides. These springs represent the contribution of the author-centred, text-centred, and listener-centred approaches and, as with the trampoline, each one works to constrain the excesses of the other on the way to a dynamic, integrated approach to the interpretation of the parables.

What are we to conclude from this story? Our images in this chapter can guide us. It is not surprising that the parables have been regarded as a novice preacher's dream and an experienced preacher's nightmare! There is so much more at work in the parable than just an earthly story with a heavenly meaning. We have glimpsed how the parable has some affinity with the allegorical story, the optical illusion, the conversation at the table, the political cartoon, the painting, and the well-told joke – and all without leaving this single means of communication. Going forward, let's reconfigure the timeline described in this chapter as a trampoline.

---

20. Zimmermann, *Puzzling the Parables*, xii.

21. Zimmermann, 11.

22. Snodgrass, *Stories with Intent*, 601. Snodgrass is considered the leading evangelical interpreter of the parables. He signals support for Zimmermann's proposal, while also posing the following key question: "Ruben Zimmermann's goal of bounded openness is correct, but how bound is the openness, and how do we know when an interpretation is out of bounds?" Snodgrass, 599.

Illustrations by Natalia De la Fuente (Cochabamba, Bolivia)

2

The Skills for Interpreting the Parables

Wilfredo Weigandt and Geoff New

When preaching the word of God, the different parts of Scripture require that we ask different questions to understand their message. We study and preach the Old Testament (OT) prophets differently to the way we approach the New Testament (NT) letters. The questions we ask of OT stories are different to those we ask of the Psalms. Similarly, when we study the parables, we need to ask the right questions if we are to preach these wondrous stories faithfully. In the OT, various sayings, riddles, poems, prophetic writings, and stories are described by the Hebrew word *mashal*. When *mashal* was translated into Greek, it became *parabolē*. "A parable is literally 'something thrown alongside of' (*para*, alongside, plus *bolē*, thrown) to which our first response is, 'What is *this* doing here?' We ask questions, we think, we imagine."[1] When we preach the parables, questions will also come to mind for our listeners. The parable will cause them to think and to imagine. During our sermon preparation, immersing ourselves in the following questions will help us to better understand the parables:

- What was happening when Jesus told this parable?
- What type of parable is this?
- What are the major themes of this parable?
- Who is the first person Jesus mentions in this parable?
- What do we need to know about the first century?
- Is there any allegory in this parable?

---

1. Peterson, *Tell It Slant*, 19.

- What is the shock in this parable?
- Does the OT provide a heritage from which this NT parable draws on?
- What difference does Jesus make?
- Am I deaf to this parable?

Let's consider these questions in more depth.

What Was Happening When Jesus Told This Parable?[2]

A sermon should reveal any important information about the first hearers of the parable, the occasion of the parable, any link between the parable and a previous story, the reason for the parable, what the parable attempts to correct or clarify, and the main teaching of the parable itself. It is also important to take special note of to whom, primarily, Jesus was speaking: The crowds? The Pharisees and scribes? The Twelve? The wider group of disciples? An individual? Such information might be given just before the parable, just after it, or both before and after. Identifying the audience will enable the preacher to discover *why* the parable was told, which helps to ensure that the sermon will be faithful to the text.

For instance, the reason Jesus related the three parables in Luke 15 (the lost sheep, the lost coin, and the lost son) was because the Pharisees and teachers of the law were grumbling about his close association with tax collectors and sinners (Luke 15:1–2). This is important information when preaching on Luke 15.

In some cases, the parable is a story which is part of a larger story. Such is the case with the first story in Luke 7:36–39 (Jesus at Simon the Pharisee's house). From this arises the second story of the two debtors (7:40–42), which in turn leads to the third story of the sinful woman being forgiven and restored (7:43–50). Together, the three stories make up the great story of Jesus's ministry recorded in Luke 7:36–50.

Another example is the parable of the good Samaritan (Luke 10:25–37). The first story deals with the question asked of Jesus by the expert in the law (10:25–29), and the parable (10:30–37) serves as the second story by which the whole story is completed. Similarly, in Luke 12:13–21, the first story is about

---

2. See "1935: The Meal and the Optical Illusion" in chapter 1, particularly the reference to the contribution made by Kenneth Bailey.

someone who wanted Jesus to settle a family dispute (12:13–15), while the second story of the rich fool (12:16–21) completes the whole story.

Some parables serve as links. For example, the story of the friend at midnight (Luke 11:5–8) – told after Jesus taught his disciples how to pray (11:1–4) and before teaching about persistence in prayer and God's goodness (11:9–13) – provides a link between what to pray for (the Lord's Prayer) and how to pray (with persistence).

Sometimes, after recording a parable, the gospel writers present important summaries that clarify Jesus's teaching or provide more insight about how the parable fits into the overall story of Jesus. For example, in recording the parable of the two sons (Matt 21:28–32) and parable of the tenants (21:33–44), Matthew concludes each one by describing how Jesus applied the parable to his audience. He also reveals the impact of these parables on the chief priests and Pharisees, who began looking for a way to arrest Jesus but refrained from doing so because they feared the crowds (21:45–46).

So, when preaching a parable, ensure that you also preach the verses surrounding the actual parable. Where there are no obvious conversations or events happening around a parable (for example, Matthew 23 and Mark 4), seek to understand why the parable has been placed at that point in the gospel. Remember, the parables were told twice: once by Jesus and then by the gospel writers.[3] Ask, "How does the placement of this parable help the overall message of this gospel?"[4]

What Type of Parable Is This?

There are different types of parables. Some are long, while others are barely one sentence. Below are the three main catgories of parables:

True-to-Life: "I'll Tell You a Story"

Some of the most familiar stories in the Bible – such as the unmerciful servant (Matt 18:21–35), the good Samaritan (Luke 10:25–37), the rich fool (Luke 12:13–21), the prodigal son (Luke 15:13–35), and Lazarus and the rich man

---

3. Snodgrass, *Stories with Intent*, 26.

4. "But just as Nathan's parable [2 Sam 12:1–7] only has force in the context of his relationship with David, so it is with Jesus's stories. They only make real sense in context." Meynell, *What Angels Long to Read*, 117.

(Luke 16:19–31) – are true-to-life parables, meaning that they describe events in daily life that Jesus's first hearers would have understood.

Chapter 3 of this book introduces a model that helps preachers to craft sermons on the parables. While this model can be used for all types of parables, true-to-life parables lend themselves most readily to this model, making the parable speak in new and wondrous ways. Applying this model to other types of parables (similitude and metaphor) proves more difficult.

Similitude: "I'll Show What It's Like"

Similitudes often begin with the statement "The kingdom of heaven (or God) is like . . ." The kingdom is compared to a common aspect of life, and this kind of parable is saying that "this everyday reality is a window into a spiritual reality." If the parable opens with the words "is like," then it is a similitude. These parables are brief.

Metaphors: "I'll Give You a Word–Picture"

Metaphors give us a new understanding about what is being talked about.[5] A metaphor describes something by using an image that is utterly different to what is being talked about. While many parables have metaphors, some parables consist solely of one or two strong metaphors. When Jesus said "You are the salt of the earth. . . . You are the light of the world" (Matt 5:13–14), he was using metaphors. People are not literally salt or light. However, these metaphors help us to understand how we must be present in the world as Jesus's disciples. Salt preserves and flavours food, and light helps people to see in the darkness; these metaphors describe the influence Jesus desires us to have in the world.

What Are the Major Themes of This Parable?

Before preaching a parable, the most important step is to identify its central idea. Most often, this is not a single, exclusive idea but a combination of several connected ideas. While the details of the story can add elements that are of

---

5. "Metaphors are very strange because when you put two things together it's a way of discovering meanings which haven't been discovered before." Walter Percy, quoted in Wiersbe, *Preaching and Teaching*, 77.

interest and value, the most important thing is to detect the story's strongest ideas and avoid getting lost in minor details that may confuse us.

For instance, to focus a sermon only on the hidden treasure (Matt 13:44) could result in a message that highlights the great worth of the kingdom. Yet, such a sermon will miss the finder's joyful, committed response to the kingdom.

When we consider the range of parables in the gospels, several common themes emerge. Some parables have more than one theme. Shown below are some of the more common themes found in the parables:

Common Themes	Example Story Lines	Example Parable
Delay	Owner going away and not returning when expected; bridegroom being delayed	Watchful servants (Luke 12:35–48)
Generosity	Workers receiving the same pay for working different hours; compassion and kindness being shown	Workers in the vineyard (Matt 20:1–16)
Faithfulness	Investing money; forgiving others	Bags of gold (Matt 25:14–30)
Judgement	Wedding banquets; harvest; fishing; weeds among wheat; wicked tenants	The net (Matt 13:47–50)
Growth of God's kingdom	Yeast; mustard seed; crops	The growing seed (Mark 4:26–29)

(Figure 1)

Each gospel writer tends to favour certain themes:
- Luke tends to favour parables of delay.
- Matthew tends to favour parables of judgement, which also tend to include dramatic scenes and characters of high status.
- Mark tends to favour farming parables.

Kingdom Themes

All parables proclaim the kingdom of God in some way. Some parables specifically begin with the words, "The kingdom of heaven [or God] is like." To discern what a parable tells us about the kingdom, we must ask:
- How does this parable shed light on Jesus as the central bearer of the kingdom?

- How does this parable show that the work of the kingdom involves both divine and human action?
- How does this parable call for action because of the kingdom?

Parables Focus on "Already" Rather Than "Not Yet"

The first recorded words of Jesus in Mark's gospel summarize the intent of the parables: "'The time has come,' he said. 'The kingdom of God has come near. Repent and believe the good news!'" (Mark 1:15).

We understand that the kingdom of God is "already but not yet." We experience the kingdom in part *now* ("already"). However, only *later*, when Jesus returns, will the kingdom come in all its fullness ("not yet"). The parables emphasize the "already" rather than the "not yet" aspect of the kingdom. They stress the urgency of responding and acting *now*. And this is important: parables demand a response from all who hear them.[6]

Who Is the First Person Jesus Mentions in This Parable?

The first person mentioned is usually (though not always) the person Jesus wants us to relate to. Consider the difference in our response when we relate to the first person mentioned in a parable.

By relating to the man who was robbed on the road to Jericho (Luke 10:30), the parable changes from whom we would give help to, to whom we would receive help from. The man who was robbed was Jewish and the only person who was helping him was a member of the hated Samaritan race. A Jew would have preferred death than receive help from a Samaritan. By relating to the character of the Jew in this parable (the first person mentioned) we can experience the challenging thought "Who would we recoil from receiving help from?"

By relating to the landowner (Matt 20:1) who pays everyone the same wage, we are challenged to consider the level of our generosity towards others in the light of the landowner's (God's) generosity.

By relating to the farmer (Mark 4:3) who scatters seed on four different types of soil, we are invited to reflect on the boundaries of where we share the word of God.

---

6. Meynell, *What Angels Long to Read*, 122.

What Do We Need to Know about the First Century?

For those living in Jesus's time, the parables were full of common things. The people, objects, animals, plants, cooking ingredients, farming practices, clothes, buildings, and other elements mentioned in the parables were part of their everyday life. "There is very little previous learning that Jesus' hearers need to bring to the occasion beyond what is gained through life experience."[7] However, the same cannot be said of twenty-first-century listeners. We have to bridge a time period of over two thousand years and a major cultural gap.

To preach so that our listeners are participants, and not merely spectators, we will need to explain those parts of the parable that will not be familiar to them. For example, in the first-century world of the NT:

- A "village" is four or six clusters of plain single-storey houses, not a rural village in the Swiss Alps with beautiful two-storey "A-frame" houses built from wood and stone with flower baskets in front of the windows. The "cities" Jesus talked about probably had twenty, forty, or even sixty thousand people living in it but not a population of twenty-one million like today's Mexico City.
- A "river" might be a wadi that is dry for most of the year and only fills up and is able to sweep away things with its current during the rainy season, utterly unlike the 40-kilometre-wide Paraná River in Argentina.
- A "road" refers to a narrow and tortuous path between desert mountains, not to a Roman military road built in Europe in the second century.
- The description "eldest son" is not merely a reference to age but signifies this son's place within the family clan and social scale in a typical rural setting.
- A "widow" does not refer merely to a woman who has lost her husband but, given a widow's lack of social protection, is an image of human vulnerability.
- Farmers first sow and then plough. Today in many parts of the world farmers plough then sow.
- Harvests, wine, and wedding banquets are symbols of the end of the age.
- The "fig-tree" and "vineyard" are pictures of Israel.

---

7. Hultgren, *Parables of Jesus*, 9.

- Finding a coin lost inside a rural house is difficult because the floors are made of stone, with large and rough joints, and often have holes. Since these houses have only a few windows – to ensure that they remained cool in summer and warm in winter – there is not much light inside.
- "Yeast" is seldom a positive image. For example, Jesus warned against the yeast of the Pharisees and Sadducees.

We study so that our listeners can also be immersed in the world of the parable. Our task is to read the parable several times to immerse ourselves in the story. This is hard, necessary, and fruitful work. A good Bible commentary will help us in this task.

We will use our imagination to picture an oriental lamp from two millennia ago and pay attention to its design, its size, its ability to radiate light, and its oil deposit. This may give us good clues to interpret the parable of the ten virgins (Matt 25:1–13). We will go to the field as we explore the parable of the weeds (Matt 13:24–30) and observe similarities and differences between the wheat and the weeds, between the size and colour of the plants, between the shape and the texture of its spikes. Perhaps then we will realize how difficult it is to discern between that which is good and bad in something during the early stages of its growth. We will imagine what it was like to go to the market and buy one hundred grams of mustard seeds (Mark 4:30–32), one hundred grams of pumpkin seeds, and one hundred grams of celery seeds. Perhaps there we will notice how tiny the mustard seed is compared to other vegetable seeds, which, when they grow, end up being much smaller plants than the mustard bush.

Not only are parables full of everyday first-century elements, they also contain symbols which served Israel's faith for thousands of years. Consider if something in the parable relates to an OT text. More than once, Jesus presented his listeners with a parable that updated ideas or texts that functioned as a common basis between them. Seek to identify where in Scripture these texts are located and keep in mind its content and interpretation. For example, in the parable of the tenants (Matt 21:33–46), which has a natural link with Isaiah 5:1–7, Jesus and his listeners shared a common base of understanding.

A parable may be connected to other NT writings. Except for the Gospel of Mark, it is possible that the Gospels were written after the Epistles, which opens up the possibility that a parable might be linked to the contents of the apostolic writings already circulating in the early church. For example,

Ephesians 2:11–22 seems to have a direct link with the parable of the tenants (Matt 21:33–46).

Is There Any Allegory in This Parable?

When symbolic or hidden meanings are given to objects or people in a parable, we call this allegory. In chapter 1, which dealt with the history of parable interpretation, we saw that for a long time allegory was the main way people understood parables. At its simplest, their approach was to see the parable as an earthly story with a heavenly meaning. While this emphasis and dominant approach to reading the parables experienced a necessary correction, allegory does play an important role in many parables. An allegory is like a code that the reader or hearer must unlock. However, unlocking the code is usually straightforward because it draws on what people are familiar with through life and faith.[8] Because the allegory is clear in what it is referring to in everyday life, "it serves to ground the story in a world familiar to the reader [and helps the reader] to explore unknown regions."[9]

An example of allegory is found in the parable of the tenants (Matt 21:33–46). In this parable, the vineyard owner is God, the vineyard represents Israel, the servants sent by the owner are the prophets, the son is Jesus, and the tenants are Israel's religious leaders. The chief priests, teachers of the law, and the elders understood exactly what Jesus meant (Mark 12:12). Other parables where allegory plays a key role include the wedding banquet (Matt 22:1–14) and the great banquet (Luke 14:16–24).

Some parables conclude with an explanation of the allegory – for example, the parables of the sower (Mark 4:13–20 and parallels), the weeds (Matt 13:36–43), and the net (Matt 13:49–50).

---

8. Kreglinger, *Storied Revelations*, 40.
9. Kreglinger, 42.

Common Allegories	Meaning	An Example Parable
Father, king	God	The two sons (Matt 21:28–31) which uses the allegory of "father" for God.
Vineyard, vines, sheep, city	Israel, covenant	The wicked tenants (Mark 12:1–12) which uses the allegory of a vineyard for Israel.
Harvest, great gathering	Final judgement	The weeds (Matt 13:24–30) which uses the allegory of a harvest for the final judgement.
Weddings, banquets, wedding robes	End of the age	The wedding banquet (Luke 14:15–24) which uses the allegory of a banquet for the end of the age.
Bridegroom, shepherd	Jesus	The ten virgins (Matt 25:1–13) which uses the allegory of a bridgegroom for Jesus.

(Figure 2)

It is important to avoid fanciful allegories. Do not apply to parts of the parable any secret and hidden meanings that do not fit with accepted biblical images or the plain sense of the passage.[10]

What Is the Shock in This Parable?

One of the unique elements of the parables is their ability to disrupt common practices and understanding. The parables are "*taken from everyday life*, but they do *not* necessarily portray everyday events."[11]

Just when the story appears to be heading towards what seems – given the customs of the dominant culture – an obvious conclusion, the disruptive element appears, causing the listener to experience sudden bewilderment, a disconcerting blow, a controversial surprise, or some form of shock at what has been heard. In some ways, the shock element in a parable works in the same way as a joke. We considered this dynamic in chapter 1, "The Story of Parable Interpretation," where we saw how a joke enjoys a "surface structure" that leads the listener along familiar lines according to "one's expectation."

---

10. When we invent hidden meanings to characters and objects in the parable, that is called allegorizing. There is a difference between allegory and allegorizing. We look for allegory as intended by Jesus when he told the parable. We avoid allegorizing, which is creating allegories which the parable does not intend.

11. Snodgrass, *Stories with Intent*, 18; emphasis in the original.

We listen to the story, thinking that we know what is coming next. However, when the punchline is delivered, we experience an invasion of the unexpected. The shock element in a parable – which is usually found at the end – works the same way.

But to understand this shock, it is necessary to understand each part of the parable according to the customs and everyday life of an ancient Middle Eastern society. If we fail to do so, that climax and rupture will go unnoticed and we will miss the vital point of the parable. In answer to the question the parable poses, we may mistakenly preach as normal what the biblical text intends to be shocking. We miss the shock because we are overfamiliar with the stories but unfamiliar with the world in which Jesus first told them.[12]

How might the Pharisees have felt when they heard Jesus identifying himself with a shepherd looking for a lost sheep or a woman looking for a lost coin? (Luke 15:3–10). In the peasant culture of the Middle East, what was the salary for a day labourer who worked a full day? The wages for one who began work at nine in the morning? For one who worked from noon? From three in the afternoon? And the one who worked from five in the afternoon for just one hour? (Matt 20:1–16). What value judgement about Jesus might Palestinian women have made as they listened to him explaining the kingdom of God using illustrations very familiar to them in the parables of the yeast, the lamp covered with a bowl, the new patch on the garment, and the ten virgins? What might have been the attitude of Palestinian vinedressers of the first century when they heard about the owner of the vineyard sending his servants to ask for his share of the harvest? How might they have felt when they heard about him sending servants a second time, in larger numbers, and, finally, even sending his own son (Matt 21:33–46)? How can it reasonably be expected that the disciples should learn from the behaviour of an unjust judge (Luke 18:1–8)? From the beginning, the judge is said to have neither feared God nor had regard for anyone else. Yet, the parable turns prior understanding upside down and teaches perseverance in prayer. What is the impact of hearing a story about a Pharisee and tax collector praying and then learning that it is the traitor who returns home justified rather than the religious leader (Luke 18:9–14)?

If we fail to get inside the skin of the first hearers and understand these situations from their perspective, we will not experience the power of confrontation that lies just beneath the surface of the parables. We will

---

12. Kreglinger, *Storied Revelations*, 208.

squash the new revelation arising and prevent the power of the symbolic from penetrating our reality.

While most parables have a shock element, some – such as the lost sheep and the lost coin (Luke 15:3–10) – do not. It is important not to try to force shock into the parable if this element is not present. However, in the absence of a shock, there might be a pleasant surprise in the parable, such as seeing ourselves as God sees us. Through the parable, we might see ourselves through the loving gaze of God. And even if there is no shock element in the parable, it may still cause shock when applied to our listeners. Strive to let the parables hit you and your listeners emotionally before they do so intellectually.[13]

Does the OT Provide a Heritage from Which the NT Parables Draw On?

Remember, the Bible Jesus grew up studying was the OT. When we preach the parables of Jesus, it helps to be familiar with OT images, symbols, and metaphors such as figs, vineyards, shepherds, wine, marriage, olives, cattle, sheep, and other everyday things that are used to convey spiritual truth.

Along with these images, symbols, and metaphors, the OT contains a range of parables. An OT parable can take the form of a proverb or a prophecy – and we see an extended example of this in Balaam's story in the book of Numbers.[14] An OT parable can take the form of a fable. A fable is a story with a clear lesson where non-human characters speak and act like people – for example, Judges 9:7–20 and 2 Kings 14:9–10, where trees and plants are the main characters. Another type of OT parable is stories, which is what we see in most of Jesus's parables. Examples of such stories in the OT include Nathan's story to King David (2 Sam 12:1–14),[15] the woman sent by Joab to King David (2 Sam 14:1–24), and the story of the vineyard told by Isaiah (Isa 5:1–7). There are also poetic parables such as Jeremiah at the potter's house (Jer 18:1–17) and Ezekiel's use of a cooking pot as an image in a parable (Ezek 24:1–14).

When reading the parables of Jesus, it is helpful to ask if he was drawing on the heritage of the OT. Are there any parts of Jesus's parable that rely on an OT image, symbol, metaphor, or parable? If so, this will help us to gain a deeper understanding of the message of the parable.

---

13. Meynell, *What Angels Long to Read*, 130.
14. Numbers 23:7–10, 18–24; 24:3–9, 15–24.
15. See chapter 8 of this book.

What Difference Does Jesus Make?

To ask what difference Jesus makes to the parable seems an unnecessary question. Jesus makes all the difference! To appreciate the importance of asking this question, reframe it in this way: "If someone other than Jesus had first told this parable, would that make a difference?"

Imagine that one of the twelve disciples had been the first to tell the parable of the good Samaritan (Luke 10:25–37). If James or John had told this story, we might be confused since they had once wanted to call down fire on a Samaritan village (Luke 9:54). If Judas had told this story, we might be sceptical, given that Judas was someone who would steal money rather than use it in the service of others (John 12:4–6). If Peter had told it, this might cloud our engagement with the parable because we know that Peter, while he often made strong statements, was also frequently wrong (Mark 8:29–33). Yet, Jesus told this parable, which makes all the difference. In a sermon on the good Samaritan, one writer beautifully illustrates the difference Jesus makes:

> There is a man who travelled that Jericho road, but in the opposite direction: toward Jerusalem, not away from it, and with a cross on his back. And from that cross the Story-teller himself repeats to us that old commandment of love.[16]

The power of the parables lie in their connection to the ministry of Jesus. We saw this in chapter 1, which surveyed how parables have been interpreted over the centuries. The connection between the parables and Jesus is also captured in the title of Snodgrass's book *Stories with Intent* – the intent of Jesus. In chapter 1, we also saw that parables must remain tied to the ministry of Jesus and his message of the kingdom of God, with that message carrying all the excitement of "pictures of revolution."[17] With such a crucial message for humanity, it should come as no surprise that one-third of Jesus's teaching was in the form of parables. Parables point to the transformation that Jesus works in people's lives.

> Jesus has not come as a religious reformer, to patch up the ragged robe of Pharisaic Judaism (foolish idea! patching would only hasten the end of the old coat). This is a new departure in the relations of God and [people]; and new especially in that His grace is exhibited to the undeserving. "The Lord loveth the righteous, and His ear is open to their cry," said the old religion. But this is

---

16. Clements, *Sting in the Tale*, 47.
17. Wenham, *Parables of Jesus*.

not now the whole story. To whom should the doctor come, if not to the sick? And so the Son of Man, in whom the Kingdom of God comes, is content to be known as "the friend of publicans and sinners." The strayed sheep is the especial object of the shepherd's care, and a frugal housewife will count no trouble too great to recover one lost coin out of her store. So Jesus went about the towns and villages of Galilee, seeking the lost; and that was how the Kingdom of God came. He launched out into the deep, and all was fish that came to His net. Nor was His appeal without results. The outcasts could be seen flocking into the Kingdom of God, as the birds fly to roost in the branches of a stalwart tree (which long ago was an almost invisible seed). And for those who accepted the Kingdom of God there was pure happiness, like the joy of a wedding feast.[18]

Put simply, Jesus makes the parable true.[19]

So, even though you are not a first-century Palestinian builder (Matt 7:24–27), sower (Mark 4:3–8), Pharisee, or tax collector (Luke 18:9–14), the parables unfold timeless truths that are intended to impact your life as a follower of Jesus Christ in the twenty-first century.

In what way do the truths that emerge from the parables affirm me as a follower of Jesus Christ? How do these parables challenge me? How do the theological principles that arise from the parables offer a corrective to the wrong attitudes of my church? What are we called to change or deepen with the help of the Holy Spirit? These values that the parables promote, how are we to apply them in the culture of our country in a way that is pleasing to God? Questions like these will help us understand the difference Jesus makes to the parables in our lives today.

This last step in our journey of studying a parable will preserve the vital, subversive, and transforming power of the parables in our own days. In chapter 1, we noted that listeners are conditioned to identify with the hero in a story. Today, we may naturally – yet mistakenly – identify with characters like the Samaritan or the tax collector. We immediately see them as the hero of the story. But when Jesus's listeners encountered such characters, their lives were subverted because they naturally and immediately saw them as the villain in

---

18. Dodd, *Parables of the Kingdom*, 148–49. This quote is part of a beautiful and extended description of Jesus's life, death, resurrection, and his teaching about the kingdom, as told using words and images from the parables.

19. Schweizer, *Luke*, 252.

the story. However, those villians became the heroes of the story. Shockingly, the expected heroes – such as a Pharisee, or priest and Levite – turn out to be the villain.

Remember that parables connect and confront. Parables are not tame – these stories are told by "the Lion of the tribe of Judah" (Rev 5:5)!

Am I Deaf to This Parable?

Our first task is to heed the lessons from the sower (Mark 4:3–9). Jesus began this parable with a command to "listen" (4:3) and concluded by saying, "Whoever has ears to hear, let them hear" (4:9). Let's take Jesus's words seriously and use the language of hearing. We are not simply reading and studying the biblical text but listening to Jesus. We are listening as we enter the first-century world of the parables so that we can preach these stories in our world. We listen carefully because most, if not all, of Jesus's parables will be familiar to us, as preachers, and to those to whom we preach. As you prepare your sermon, seek to hear the parable as if for the first time. One NT scholar writes that "one of the most striking things about the parables of Jesus is their directness of address to the audience."[20] While all parables have this feature, it is especially evident in some. For example, some parables have direct challenges: "Which of you?" (Matt 7:9); "What do you think?" (Matt 18:12); "Who then is the faithful and wise servant?" (Matt 24:45); "Suppose one of you" (Luke 14:28).[21] To feel the weight of the parable's message and hear it in its purest tones, we need to clear the rubble from our soul – the kind of rubble that collects from being overfamiliar with the parables, bored with them, or assuming that they have nothing new to say to us; the kind of rubble that collects when we try to tame the parables and reduce them to our way of thinking and our way of doing things.

So, let's take the parable away from the markets of Mumbai and Mogadishu. Let's get the parable out of our pastoral offices in Melbourne or Moscow. Let's remove it from the busy streets of Medellin or Medan. Let's not allow it to be coloured by the economies of Maracay or Multan. Let's take away the aroma of a pulpit in Manchester or Manila. Let's not leave the parable to the mercy of the customs of a church in Minneapolis or Milan.

---

20. Hultgren, *Parables of Jesus*, 8.
21. Other examples include Matthew 5:24; 7:9; 12:11; 21:28; Luke 11:5, 11; 12:42; 14:31; 15:4, 8; 17:7.

Instead, let's place the parable in the Israel of David, the Judah of Jeremiah, and the Palestine of Jesus. Let's place these stories called parables where they flowed naturally, where they were believable, where they first found their home. We will try to get into the history of the parable. We will try to go through these stories like a farmer from the Middle East. We will try to inhabit the parable as invisible guests. We will try to feel these stories from the hearts of those who first heard them two thousand years ago. We will try to recreate these parables by our most sincere efforts. We will try.

This will be the beginning of our preaching journey: a challenge to perceive the parables in the settings in which the Scriptures present them. But how do we start on this journey? By remembering our task of interpretating parables for preaching is a spiritual one. When studying a parable, imagine that Jesus is seated opposite you as a friend telling you the story. Hear it as for the first time and let it impact you as his disciple. "Whoever has ears to hear, let them hear."

3

Picture-Mirror-Window-Door

Geoff New

Chapter 1 considered the different ways the church has read the parables over the centuries. Chapter 2 highlighted what to look for in a parable when preparing a sermon. This chapter explains a simple way to study the parables, and chapters 4–7 will bring all this information together and describe how to use this model in the preparation and delivery of a sermon.

In his book *Preaching and Teaching with Imagination: The Quest for Biblical Ministry*, Warren Wiersbe describes his approach to engaging with the parables: "I like to think of a parable as a *picture* that becomes a *mirror* and then a *window*."[1] Wiersbe explains his model like this:[2]

> A parable starts out as a picture of something in life, something recognizable that at the same time contains something different. . . . The longer we look at the "parable picture," the more it becomes a mirror *and we start to see ourselves*. . . . Jesus didn't simply use parables as "illustrations," the way preachers tell stories to explain their points, but as *illumination*, the kind of light that pierced the very hearts and minds of listeners and made them aware of their

---

1. Wiersbe, *Preaching and Teaching*, 164; emphasis in the original. Similar approaches to Wiersbe's model can be found in various publications, with authors sometimes building on one another's work as they develop their own models. Some works are academic, while others are written for day-to-day ministry. See, for example, Krieger, *Window*, who develops a window-mirror-window model; Via, *The Parables*; Hughes, "Preaching the Parables," which offers a helpful summary; and Bowling, *Windows and Mirrors*. See also Brueggemann, *Spirituality of the Psalms*. While Brueggemann's focus is on the psalms, his mapping of the book of Psalms as orientation-disorientation-reorientation speaks into the kind of model we are working with in this book. Brueggemann applies his model to Jesus's suffering, crucifixion, and resurrection and, in so doing, inspires reflection on other aspects of Jesus's ministry such as the parables.

2. Wiersbe, *Preaching and Teaching*, 165; emphasis in the original.

needs.... But that isn't the end: the mirror must then become a window *so that the listeners see God and His truth and receive the message by faith.* Our Lord's enemies never got to this third stage. Having seen themselves reflected, they then tried to break the mirror by resisting the truth. The "shock of recognition" was too much for them.

By expanding the model beyond the third stage (the window), we can experience even more of the parable's impact. Beyond this window stands a door, and through the door lies the path of discipleship in Christ. Beyond the door lies life that is deepened and defined by the parable at hand.

In our sermon preparation, we move through each of these four stages or movements: Picture, Mirror, Window, and Door. In preaching a parable, these four movements shape our sermon. We can describe the four movements as shown in the chart below:

When preaching a parable, look...[3]			
at the Picture	*in* the Mirror	*through* the Window	*beyond* the Door
We see life	We see ourselves	We see God	We see others
Sight	Insight	Vision	Imagination
Information	Intimidation	Invitation	Incarnation
Somebody else	Me!	God and me	God, me, and others
I'm interested	I'm shattered	I'm challenged	I'm called
Knowledge	Conviction	Revelation	Response

(Figure 3)

When preparing a sermon on a parable, we progress through the stages in order: Picture, Mirror, Window, and Door. In each movement, our focus changes. Figure 3 offers descriptions of the effect a parable can have during each of these stages. Each line of the chart lists responses and experiences that relate to the different stages of looking at the picture, in the mirror, through the window, and beyond the door of the parable. How the parable works in this way holds true during both sermon preparation *and* sermon delivery. As our listeners hear the sermon, they will also experience the parable as a picture, which becomes a mirror, then a window, and, finally, a door.

---

3. Adapted from Wiersbe, 165. For another use of Wiersbe's model for preaching, readers might be interested in reading Woods, *God is in the House*, 93–113.

A summary of this process will help us to understand how it works. In the first stage, we study the parable as a picture. We gaze at the picture to observe it closely. We seek to understand how the parable is a picture of life in first-century Palestine. Here, we unpack the characters, objects, location, and action in the parable. We explain how this parable describes everyday life in Jesus's time. Some aspects of this picture may also relate to our lives today. For example, in the parable of the Pharisee and the tax collector (Luke 18:9–14), we might recognize that such attitudes to prayer are also prevalent in our worship settings today. In Figure 4, under the heading "*at* the Picture," we might realize that the line "We see life" best sums up our study.

When preaching a parable, look...			
at the Picture	*in* the Mirror	*through* the Window	*beyond* the Door
We see life	We see ourselves	We see God	We see others

(Figure 4)

In the second stage, we look at the parable as we would look in a mirror. We see our reflection in the parable. Our focus turns to what the parable says to us and what it reveals about our life. The first stage (picture) focused on life two thousand years ago. Now, in the mirror stage, the focus is on our life today. The reflection we see in the mirror of the parable might prove confrontational and even shocking. In Figure 5, under the heading "*in* the Mirror," the line "We see ourselves" sums up this stage.

When preaching a parable, look...			
at the Picture	*in* the Mirror	*through* the Window	*beyond* the Door
We see life	We see ourselves	We see God	We see others

(Figure 5)

In the third stage, we look at the parable as we would look through a window. The parable gives us a new vision, whereby we see and experience God differently. The view through the window of the parable may challenge what we had previously understood about God. We may see new things, and we may see God in new ways. In Figure 6, under the heading "*through* the Window," our encounter is described by the words "We see God."

When preaching a parable, look . . .			
at the Picture	*in* the Mirror	*through* the Window	*beyond* the Door
We see life	We see ourselves	We see God	We see others

(Figure 6)

The fourth stage requires that we look at the parable as we would look at a door. The door presents a new way of living with God and in this world. Here, our study uncovers how we are to live anew as citizens of the kingdom. The door of the parable offers a new way to live according to the Scriptures. We are inspired to expand our hearts and minds, and live more fully in Christ. In Figure 7, under the heading "*beyond* the Door," the words "We see others" rounds off our engagement with the parable.

When preaching a parable, look . . .			
at the Picture	*in* the Mirror	*through* the Window	*beyond* the Door
We see life	We see ourselves	We see God	We see others

(Figure 7)

To summarize, each line of the chart offers different descriptions of how a parable works as a Picture, a Mirror, a Window, and a Door. While it is more straightforward to stay on the same line as you work through these four elements, if you prefer, you can use a description from a different line as you progress through the four movements.[4] The important thing is to use those descriptions which best capture what the Spirit is saying to you as you prepare your sermon. As you become more familiar with this model, you are encouraged to create your own descriptions in your study of the parables.

---

4. This will be demonstrated in chapters 8–15, which contain sample sermons.

Part 1

4

Look *at* the Picture

Geoff New

Now let's spend time studying a parable and using the Picture-Mirror-Window-Door model for sermon preparation and delivery.

The gospel writer Luke provides us with a rich account of a time Jesus accepted an invitation to a meal at a Pharisee's home (Luke 7:36–50). The events that took place at this meal resulted in Jesus telling the parable of the two debtors. Jesus not only told this parable but applied it to the people who were listening to it. The way Jesus applied this parable helps us to see clearly how parables work according to the Picture-Mirror-Window-Door model.

Luke 7:36–50

> [36] When one of the Pharisees invited Jesus to have dinner with him, he went to the Pharisee's house and reclined at the table. [37] A woman in that town who lived a sinful life learned that Jesus was eating at the Pharisee's house, so she came there with an alabaster jar of perfume. [38] As she stood behind him at his feet weeping, she began to wet his feet with her tears. Then she wiped them with her hair, kissed them and poured perfume on them.
>
> [39] When the Pharisee who had invited him saw this, he said to himself, "If this man were a prophet, he would know who is touching him and what kind of woman she is – that she is a sinner."
>
> [40] Jesus answered him, "Simon, I have something to tell you."
>
> "Tell me, teacher," he said.
>
> [41] "Two people owed money to a certain money-lender. One owed him five hundred denarii, and the other fifty. [42] Neither of

them had the money to pay him back, so he forgave the debts of both. Now which of them will love him more?"

⁴³ Simon replied, "I suppose the one who had the bigger debt forgiven."

"You have judged correctly," Jesus said.

⁴⁴ Then he turned towards the woman and said to Simon, "Do you see this woman? I came into your house. You did not give me any water for my feet, but she wet my feet with her tears and wiped them with her hair. ⁴⁵ You did not give me a kiss, but this woman, from the time I entered, has not stopped kissing my feet. ⁴⁶ You did not put oil on my head, but she has poured perfume on my feet. ⁴⁷ Therefore, I tell you, her many sins have been forgiven – as her great love has shown. But whoever has been forgiven little loves little."

⁴⁸ Then Jesus said to her, "Your sins are forgiven."

⁴⁹ The other guests began to say among themselves, "Who is this who even forgives sins?"

⁵⁰ Jesus said to the woman, "Your faith has saved you; go in peace."

Our first task is to look at the picture this parable presents. We need to paint this picture for our listeners. We read, study, and observe the Scripture carefully and deeply. Our focus in this part of our sermon preparation is Luke 7:36–42. These verses describe Jesus dining at the Pharisee's house, the woman anointing Jesus's feet, the Pharisee's private thoughts about this incident, and the parable that Jesus told in response. We will consider the remaining verses (7:43–50) when we look in the mirror, through the window, and beyond the door.

To look at this parable as a picture, we must answer the questions that were outlined in chapter 2 of this book (*The Skills for Interpreting the Parables*).

Am I Deaf to This Parable?

Jesus began this parable by directly addressing Simon: "Simon, I have something to tell you" (7:40). As you begin to look at the picture, Jesus says to you, "I have something to tell you. Are you listening?" The parable concludes with a question that demands a response (7:42). This question emphasizes the importance of listening, which is a feature of all parables: "Listen!" (Mark 4:3).

What Was Happening When Jesus Told This Parable?

Luke provides us with information about what happened before and after the parable was told. We notice that the parable of the two debtors is the middle story in the three stories contained in Luke 7:36–50. The first story describes Jesus being invited to the Pharisee's house, eating a meal, the woman anointing his feet, and the Pharisee objecting to her actions (7:36–39); the second story is the telling of the parable of the two debtors (7:40–42); and the third story tells us what Jesus said and did after telling the parable (7:43–50). To preach this parable effectively, all three stories need to be part of the sermon. The parable only gives its full sense when the events surrounding it are also explained.

What Type of Parable Is This?

This parable is "true-to-life." It describes something that is part of everyday life – a person in debt. However, as is often the case with parables, what happens is not an everyday occurrence – the debt is cancelled. In the story of the two debtors, we notice a feature that is common in parables found in the Gospel of Luke. Luke has several parables which begin with words to the effect "a certain man" or "suppose one of you." The two debtors begins with a "certain money-lender" (7:42), which has the effect of widening the invitation into the story. Since this has the effect of saying "someone" or "anyone," listeners can more easily see themselves in the story.[1]

What Are the Major Themes of This Parable?

The major theme of this parable is generosity, as shown by the money-lender. When applying this theme of generosity to the situation of the Pharisee and the woman, Jesus introduced further themes: sin, divine forgiveness, and love. We see the kingdom theme of the connection between divine and human performance. God forgives (divine performance) and those forgiven respond with love (human performance). Connected with this is the call to action – in the form of forgiveness of sin – because of the kingdom being "already." How will those who have enjoyed God's forgiveness relate to other sinners who have also been forgiven?

---

1. Snodgrass, *Stories with Intent*, 12. For example, the good Samaritan (Luke 10:30), the friend at midnight (Luke 11:5), the lost sheep (Luke 15:4), the lost coin (Luke 15:8), and the lost son (Luke 15:11) start with "a certain man/woman" or "suppose one of you/who among you."

Who Is the First Person Jesus Mentions in This Parable?

Some Bible versions mention the money-lender first, while others first refer to the two people who owe him money. Bible commentaries confirm that the money-lender is the first person mentioned. By saying that "a man loaned money to two people" (7:41 NLT), Jesus wanted his listeners to first relate to the money-lender – that is, the person to whom others are in debt. The money-lender represents God, and Jesus's focus was the debt due to God because of humanity's sin.

What Do We Need to Know about the First Century?

The parable itself is a simple story, and the events before and after its telling appear straightforward. However, when painting the picture for our audience, there are many features of the first century that we, as preachers, must be aware of. We need to "breathe the air of first-century Judaism"[2] to ensure that we are hearing the parable as Jesus intended.

Luke writes that Jesus "reclined at the table" (7:36), which describes how people of that time participated in a meal – they would lie on their left side, with their legs stretched out behind them.[3] The feet were always placed behind "because of the offensive, unclean nature of feet in Oriental society from time immemorial until the present."[4] This was why the woman was able to anoint Jesus's feet as he ate.

The woman arrived with an alabaster jar of perfume (7:37). Olive oil was usually used to anoint a person's feet because it was cheap. However, the woman used an expensive perfume, which had been stored in a jar to preserve its quality.[5] The cost of such perfume – probably nard – could amount to as much as a year's wages. The neck of the jar would be broken to pour out the perfume.

To dry Jesus's feet with her hair, the woman would have had to let her hair down (7:38), which, in that culture, was equivalent to being in a state of undress in public.[6] Indeed, rabbis of the time were of the view that if a woman let her hair down in the presence of another man, this was grounds for divorce.[7]

---

2. Snodgrass, 178.
3. Green, *Luke*, 310.
4. Bailey, *Through Peasant Eyes*, 5.
5. Bock, *Luke*, 696.
6. Green, *Luke*, 310.
7. Bailey, *Through Peasant Eyes*, 9.

A guest would never, under any circumstances, criticize a host's hospitality.[8] Indeed, the custom was that guests would repeatedly say how unworthy they were to have been shown hospitality, no matter how inadequate such hospitality had been. So, for Jesus to not only point out Simon's lack of hospitality but do so in such a critical way would have been astonishing in that culture.

The woman was obviously uninvited and unwelcome. However, "that the woman's action is rebuked and her presence is not suggests a special, public meal."[9] On such occasions, the doors were left open and uninvited guests could sit against the wall and listen in. The meal relied on ritual purity to decide who could be there and what could be eaten. At such meals a visiting teacher was invited and religious discussion about an issue took place.

While the parable is about two people owing money and was told, primarily, to Simon, others present at the banquet would also have related to the story. Attending a meal such as this would have placed the guests in debt to the host. Payment would be expected later in some way.[10]

Is There Any Allegory in This Parable?

Remember, an allegory is like a code, where the person hearing the parable needs to unlock the code. This is usually simple because it draws on what is familiar in life and faith. Jesus's application of the parable (7:44–47) makes it clear that the money-lender is God, the debt is sin, and the two debtors are Simon and the woman.

Where Is the Shock in This Parable?

The shock in this parable lies in the fact that a money-lender forgave a debt. Lending money and earning interest from such loans is a money-lender's business. To forgive a debt means losing his money and the interest he would have gained from the repayments. Such a practice would give rise to other potential problems for the money-lender: What message would this convey to others who owed him money? Would it raise their expectations that their debts would also be forgiven? Would other people try to take advantage of the money-lender's generosity? While it could result in more business for him, it could also mean more people hoping that they would never have to pay back their loans.

---

8. Bailey, 14–15.
9. Bock, *Luke*, 694–95.
10. Green, *Luke*, 311.

What Difference Does Jesus Make?

Jesus makes the parable true. If the woman had not been present, Jesus would not have told the story. Without Jesus, the woman would not have acted the way she did. Another feature that emphasizes the significance of Jesus's ministry is that he told the parable in response to what the Pharisee *thought* (7:39). Luke records that Jesus "answered" Simon (7:40) even though Simon had not said anything aloud.

With this parable, Jesus described what he perceived (Simon's thoughts), saw (the woman), experienced (the woman attending him) and gifted (forgiveness of sins) at that meal in Simon's house. Without Jesus's ministry of taking away the sin of the world, this parable would not be true. Jesus defines what it means to take away sin and completes the picture by taking away the sins of the woman.

Summary

Through the exercise of looking "*at* the Picture" of this parable in its setting, we have experienced what is listed under the heading "*at* the Picture" in the first column of the chart below (Figure 8). "We see life" in the first century, our "Sight" has cleared, we have gained "Information," we have heard a story about "Somebody else," we are "interested," and we now have new "Knowledge."

However, in preparing our sermon, it is best to settle on just one of these descriptions to give our sermon focus. After studying and observing the biblical text, we look at the chart (Figure 8) and decide which description best sums up our study after having looked "*at* the Picture." For the purpose of illustrating how to use the chart, we will use the second line of descriptions. So, by gazing at the picture of the two debtors through careful observation of the text (7:36–42), we have gained "Sight."

When preaching a parable, look . . .			
at the Picture	*in* the Mirror	*through* the Window	*beyond* the Door
We see life	We see ourselves	We see God	We see others
Sight	Insight	Vision	Imagination
Information	Intimidation	Invitation	Incarnation
Somebody else	Me!	God and me	God, me, and others
I'm interested	I'm shattered	I'm challenged	I'm called
Knowledge	Conviction	Revelation	Response

(Figure 8)

With our new "Sight" related to this portion of Scripture, we have material to use in our sermon to paint the picture for our listeners. But now there is a change. The picture of The Two Debtors becomes a mirror and in Luke 7:43–47, Jesus shows us how this change takes place. Our attention now turns to this.

Worksheet for "Picture"

Scan the QR Code for a worksheet to help you look at the picture of the parable.

https://bit.ly/PtP-Picture

5

Look *in* the Mirror

Geoff New

The first stage of our study of the two debtors involved looking "*at* the Picture" and deciding to use the description from the second line in the chart: "Sight" (see Figure 9 below). That picture involved looking at the events at the meal table and the parable itself. The two debtors is a brief and simple story, told in two or three sentences. "Parables appear in quick, precise strokes. A parable is feeble; almost all the power is in the one who hears it."[1] This power that lies with the hearer of the parable is evident in the way Jesus concluded the parable with a question. Of the two debtors who had their loans forgiven by the money-lender, "which of them will love him more?" (Luke 7:42). With this question, the parable changes from a picture to a mirror. What does Simon see in the mirror? What will we and our listeners see?

We look "*in* the Mirror" and receive "Insight."

When preaching a parable, look . . .			
at the Picture	*in* the Mirror	*through* the Window	*beyond* the Door
Sight	Insight	Vision	Imagination

(Figure 9)

As we gaze in the mirror, with a view to inviting others to do so as well, we are required to study the biblical text and discern what the Spirit is saying to the church. We study how it worked as a mirror two thousand years ago in Simon's life and discern how it works as a mirror in our lives today. For this stage in our sermon preparation, we need spiritual wisdom. Given that

---

1. Sulivan, *Morning Light*, 64, quoted in Peterson, *Tell It Slant*, 19.

almost all the power of the parable rests with the one who hears it, our sermon needs to be crafted so that our hearers are enabled to see their reflection in the parable. This requires sermon content that guides this process of reflection and facilitates the work of the Spirit. The way Jesus applied the two debtors to Simon provides us with guidance on how to prepare and preach this part of our sermon as a mirror.

The answer to the question "Now which of them will love him more?" (7:42) is obvious, and Simon is trapped. He answers, "I suppose the one who had the bigger debt forgiven" (7:43). Simon's opening words, "I suppose," comes across as reluctant, if not resentful. He knows where this is heading and he does not like it. Simon has caught a glimpse of his reflection in the mirror. Jesus replies, "You have judged correctly" (7:43). As seen in Luke's description of the day's events, a lot has been going on in Simon's heart and mind. Jesus's first recorded words are in the telling of the parable of the two debtors, followed by his confirmation that Simon has answered correctly. Simon's reflection in the mirror is becoming sharper.

The events of Luke 7:36–50 show us the pace we must adopt in preaching a parable. As with Jesus's interaction with Simon, our aim, at this point in our sermon, must be to create space for our listeners so that they can look in the mirror. Note the important silences and gaps in the events described in Luke 7:36–50.

There is the silence and gap of Simon's hospitality to Jesus. One verse tells of Simon's invitation, and Jesus's acceptance of it and his arrival at the Pharisee's house (7:36). No details are given about how Jesus was received by Simon. Such details would come later, when Jesus addresses Simon's lack of hospitality (7:44–46). There is Jesus's silence when the woman anoints him – Jesus allows this to happen without a word being spoken. One commentator makes the point that Luke describes each act of the woman – wiping, kissing, anointing – in a way that conveys that this would have taken some time.[2] Jesus remains silent throughout, and his silence is matched by Simon's silence. While Simon speaks to himself, he does not speak aloud to Jesus or to the woman about his distaste about what is happening. Jesus tells the parable only after the woman has done something and after Simon has thought something. This perfect timing of the parable breaks the silence. Of course, we cannot time our sermon to happen just after someone has done something and someone else has entertained unkind thoughts; nevertheless, in our preaching, we must rely on the Spirit to ensure that our sermon is a word in season.

---

2. Bock, *Luke*, 697.

When Jesus tells the parable in response to Simon's thoughts, a kind of silence continues. Jesus relates this story in such a way that it delays the moment of confrontation. By beginning the parable with a call for Simon's attention – "Simon, I have something to tell you" (7:40) – and finishing with a question – "Now which of them will love him more?" (7:42) – Jesus creates time and space for Simon to fall into the parable. A response is demanded of Simon. We do well to craft our sermons by imitating Jesus's approach. Guard against over-explaining how the parable applies to your listeners too early in your sermon. Leave room for the parable to do its work, and let people wrestle with what it means. Leave room for the parable to demand a response from its hearers for there are spaces in the parable for them to enter the story. Leave room for your listeners to gaze in the mirror of the parable.

The spaces in the parables are created by a common feature of parables – they often lack details and, therefore, contain silences. While we need to be careful not to make too much of such silences, there is value in being aware of these gaps. Often, the shock element of the parable opens up such gaps and silences. As we saw in chapter 3, the shock in the parable of the two debtors is that a money-lender would forgive a debt. Such a shocking twist in the story raises questions: What would it mean for others who owed that lender money? Would it raise their expectations that their debts would also be forgiven? Would other people try to take advantage of the money-lender's generosity? These questions are not answered in the parable, but the parable works in a way that causes our hearts and minds to ponder such things. The parable raises outrageous possibilities. "A parable's omissions are deliberate. . . . [they] are openings, silent rooms for listeners to enter for confrontation, consideration, and response, for offering speech of their own. They are empty spaces for the Spirit."[3] When we honour these silent rooms and empty spaces in our sermon, our listeners are more likely to hear the parable as those who are personally involved rather than as those who remain untouched by the parable. They are more likely to see their reflection in the mirror, and, as in Simon's case, this reflection in the mirror becomes sharper.

So, with the two debtors, the questions raised by the shock element result in what we were already alerted to in chapter 1 – that is, C. H. Dodd's insight that the shock element results in "leaving the mind in sufficient doubt about its precise application to tease it into active thought."[4] The silences and gaps

---

3. Duke, *Parables*, 101.

4. Dodd, *Parables of the Kingdom*, 16. This quote is part of C. H. Dodd's classic definition of a parable: "At its simplest the parable is a metaphor or simile drawn from nature or common life, arresting the hearer by its vividness or strangeness, and leaving the mind in sufficient doubt

might be filled with various considerations and confrontations: What does this parable reveal about our church community? Do I have any sense of having a great debt forgiven in my life? If so, is my response one that Jesus would commend? Do I simply assume that my debt will be forgiven and, therefore, fail to show gratitude? Am I even aware of my debt to God? Having honoured the silences and spaces for the Spirit to speak, we then attend to the work of commenting about what we see in the mirror. Again, Jesus's example must inspire us. Jesus polished the mirror for Simon to look into.

Luke 7:44–46

> ⁴⁴ Then he [Jesus] turned towards the woman and said to Simon, "Do you see this woman? I came into your house. You did not give me any water for my feet, but she wet my feet with her tears and wiped them with her hair. ⁴⁵ You did not give me a kiss, but this woman, from the time I entered, has not stopped kissing my feet. ⁴⁶ You did not put oil on my head, but she has poured perfume on my feet."

Jesus begins by directing Simon's attention to the woman: "Then he turned towards the woman and said to Simon, 'Do you see this woman?'" (7:44). In doing this, Jesus dignifies the woman and confronts Simon. Until this point, Simon had thought that he had seen the woman. In his eyes, she is sinful and unwelcome. She is ritually unclean, and Simon thinks that someone of Jesus's status should not even let her near him. By asking "Do you see this woman?" Jesus clears Simon's vision.

Jesus polishes the mirror by identifying the two debtors in the room. Simon has no choice but to look "*in* the Mirror." He sees reflected there his attitudes and actions. Jesus describes what had happened from the time he entered Simon's house. As the host, Simon had neglected his responsibilities towards his guest. Whether or not Simon deliberately withheld hospitality is uncertain, but what is certain is that this lack of hospitality dishonoured Jesus, who was his guest. Jesus compares Simon's lack of attention to the woman's devoted attention. He begins, "I came into your house" (7:44) and then, three times, points out what Simon "did not" do: "You did not give me any water for my feet . . . You did not give me a kiss . . . You did not put oil on my head." In contrast, Jesus affirms that the woman "wet my feet with her tears and wiped

---

about its precise application to tease it into active thought."

them with her hair . . . has not stopped kissing my feet . . . has poured perfume on my feet" (7:44–46).

Simon had earlier sneered at the woman's attention towards Jesus. Simon is blind to her act of devotion and its significance. He sees nothing other than a sinful woman "touching" (7:39) his guest, who was supposed to be a prophet. In Simon's eyes, nothing is right about the scene. The sinful woman's actions are an embarrassment, and Jesus's apparent lack of recognition of her sin disqualifies him, in Simon's eyes, as a prophet. However, Jesus defines and honours the woman's actions. In contrast to Simon's one-word summary of events ("touching"), Jesus gives a full commentary – tears, wiping with her hair, kissing his feet, pouring perfume – that applauds the woman's actions. Simon sees a woman who is empty by his standards. Jesus confronts Simon with a mirror that shows him who is really empty. Simon's emptiness is seen in the description of him as "the Pharisee who had invited Jesus" (7:36, 39). No other words are used to describe his hosting because there is nothing to report. Simon had invited Jesus; Jesus had arrived and begun to eat; Simon had not greeted Jesus with a kiss, anointed him, or washed his feet. To fail to wash a guest's feet was to convey the message that the person was considered inferior. "The insult to Jesus has to be intentional and electrifies the assembled guests. War has been declared and everyone waits to see Jesus' response."[5] At first, Jesus had remained silent. The woman's acts of hospitality filled in the gaps (7:38). Only as Jesus describes the reflection in the mirror does Simon see her love for Jesus and recognize his own neglect of Jesus.

Simon's emptiness is also seen in the initial absence of names in the telling of the story. Four times, Simon remains unnamed and is referred to as "the Pharisee" (7:36, 37, 39); and Simon, in his negative thoughts, refers to Jesus merely as "this man" (7:39). When Jesus holds up the mirror of his parable, Simon is named for the first time (7:40). Thereafter, he is no longer referred to as "the Pharisee" but is identified by name. This adds to the sense of personal confrontation and the responsibility to hear the parable and understand its message.

In our sermon, in this second stage of looking "*in* the Mirror," we must allow time for the Spirit to engage listeners in the silent rooms and empty spaces in the parable. "The gaps force the reader to fill in the blanks . . . to begin to ask questions, to search for justifications and arguments, and perhaps also – as is demonstrated by the story – to be affected emotionally."[6] We then

---

5. Bailey, *Through Peasant Eyes*, 8.
6. Zimmermann, *Puzzling the Parables*, 156–57.

rely on the Spirit to equip us to carefully communicate the reflection in the mirror in the manner that Jesus did with Simon.

Summary

The two debtors works like the parable Nathan told King David (2 Sam 12:1–4). A parable is something that we fall into.[7] "For a parable is not an explanation. A parable is not an illustration. We cannot look at a parable as a spectator and expect to get it. A parable does not make a thing easier; it makes it harder by requiring participation, by entering the story."[8] A parable reflects how we are living before God and with others. The image in the mirror is confronting. In chapter 2, we saw that the first person mentioned in a parable is often the person Jesus wants us to relate to. The money-lender (God) is the first person mentioned in this story. Of the two debtors, the first one mentioned is the one with the greater debt (the woman). Like King David, centuries before him, Simon is shown that he is the lesser character in the story. Simon discovers that parables connect with human experience "but by mirroring they seek to change behaviour and create disciples. *Their main purpose is to goad* [provoke] *people into response.*"[9] The way Jesus holds up the mirror of the two debtors for Simon is masterful. So, in our preaching, after encouraging our listeners to look "*at* the Picture," we then face the challenge of preaching so that our listeners can look "*in* the Mirror."

With reference to our chart (Figure 10), our first view of the parable as a picture, which gave us "Sight," now changes to a mirror in which we receive "Insight."

When preaching a parable, look . . .			
at the Picture	*in* the Mirror	*through* the Window	*beyond* the Door
We see life	We see ourselves	We see God	We see others
Sight	Insight	Vision	Imagination
Information	Intimidation	Invitation	Incarnation
Somebody else	Me!	God and me	God, me, and others
I'm interested	I'm shattered	I'm challenged	I'm called
Knowledge	Conviction	Revelation	Response

(Figure 10)

---

7. Kruschwitz, "How (Not) to Read," 257.
8. Peterson, *Tell It Slant*, 59–60.
9. Snodgrass, *Stories with Intent*, 18; emphasis in the original.

For the purposes of learning this model, we are using the second line in the chart. However, it is entirely possible that through your study of the parable you find a description on a different line more fitting. Remember, not all parables have a shock element or will shock all listeners. While the two debtors would have shocked the Pharisee, the woman would have been pleasantly surprised by this story. The same can happen to us and our listeners – some may be shocked, while others are encouraged. So, under the heading "*in* the Mirror," you might decide that "We see ourselves" is more accurate because you became aware of seeing yourself through God's loving gaze. During your study, by the work of the Spirit, you might have experienced "Intimidation" or found your heart crying I see "Me!" in the mirror. Perhaps you were shocked at what you saw and the phrase "I'm shattered!" better reflects this part of your sermon preparation. Still others may experience "Conviction." Settle on that description of the mirror that seems to fit best. Remember, the important thing is to listen to the parable and preach what you hear.

Now we turn our gaze to the third stage: looking "*through* the Window."

Worksheet for "Mirror"

Scan the QR Code for a worksheet to help you look in the mirror of the parable.

https://bit.ly/PtP-Mirror

6

Look *Through* the Window

Geoff New

Jesus's telling of the two debtors shows how a parable works as a picture which becomes a mirror. As Simon responded to the picture of the parable (Luke 7:43), Jesus held it up as a mirror to show Simon his lack of hospitality and love (7:44–46). The reflection in the mirror also shows the woman extravagantly making up for Simon's lack of attention towards Jesus. In our sermon preparation so far, by looking at the picture of the two debtors, we received "Sight," and by looking in the mirror, we received "Insight." In Luke 7:47–49, we see how the parable now becomes a window.

Luke 7:47–49

> ⁴⁷ "Therefore, I tell you, her many sins have been forgiven – as her great love has shown. But whoever has been forgiven little loves little."
> ⁴⁸ Then Jesus said to her, "Your sins are forgiven."
> ⁴⁹ The other guests began to say among themselves, "Who is this who even forgives sins?"

As we look "*through* the Window," we receive "Vision."

When preaching a parable, look...			
at the Picture	*in* the Mirror	*through* the Window	*beyond* the Door
Sight	Insight	Vision	Imagination

(Figure 11)

With his words, "I tell you, her many sins have been forgiven – as her great love has shown," Jesus directs Simon's, the woman's, the guests', and our gaze through the window. There we see the vision of someone who has experienced the love of God and returned that love. The only detail given about the woman's sins are that they were many. Although Luke does not mention the nature of her sins, it is clear that they were of the kind that resulted in a bad reputation in the community.[1] She was ritually unclean, and her touch would make another person unclean. But now, with Jesus, all that changed.

Jesus speaks to Simon and shows him the vision through the window created by the parable of the two debtors. The woman has a new status – forgiven – and she also enjoys a new reputation – one who has shown great love towards God (7:47). The view through the window also shows Simon's status: "But whoever has been forgiven little loves little" (7:47). Simon's reputation is in stark contrast to that of the woman, whose very presence offended him. That he has been forgiven little does not mean that Simon's sins are little. It is more likely that Simon has little awareness of the extent of his sin and has not repented.[2] Through the window of this parable, the woman is seen as more and Simon is seen as less. Jesus speaks to the woman and shows her the vision through the window created by the telling of the two debtors. She now has a new life, and her past no longer defines her (7:48).

The guests talk among themselves. Since Simon was a Pharisee, it is reasonable to assume that other Pharisees would have been among his guests. They, too, see a new vision through the window created by the story of the two debtors, and they are astonished – and probably offended – at what seems blasphemous.[3] They say among themselves, "Who is this who even forgives sins?" (7:49). Through the window, they see Jesus as the forgiver of sins. How is that possible? For only God can forgive sin. The vision through the window, as it relates to Jesus, is huge. "Who is this?!"

Together, the community at that meal hear Jesus's words and, through the window, see a vision of the kingdom of God here and now in their town. Each person sees the same thing, yet each is impacted differently. For some, this is good news because they have a vision of new life through God's acceptance. For others, it is confronting news because this vision of Jesus goes beyond

---

1. Most Bible commentators say it is reasonable to assume that her sin was sexual and that she was either a prostitute or had lived a life that was sexually immoral.
2. Bailey, *Through Peasant Eyes*, 18.
3. Compare Luke 5:16–26. "When Jesus saw their faith, he said, 'Friend, your sins are forgiven.' The Pharisees and the teachers of the law began thinking to themselves, 'Who is this fellow who speaks blasphemy? Who can forgive sins but God alone?'" (5:20–21).

how they had previously seen him. Simon, who had earlier viewed Jesus as a "prophet" (7:39) and "teacher" (7:40), now sees him as one who forgives sin. Jesus claims divine status. This is challenging news for everyone because it redefines their vision of community life before God.

When preparing and preaching a sermon, our task is to direct our listeners' gaze through the window. In Luke 7:36–50, there are three main characters or groups hearing the two debtors. As we have seen, they each see something different through the window. When we preach, we, together with our listeners, form yet another group or become as one of the characters; and, therefore, we become as those who need to hear the parable as much as the first hearers. Just as each of them were affected differently by the parable, we need to allow the Spirit to open our eyes to a new vision through the window. "Parables are full of trap doors into another world, another vantage point, another focus, another insight into what we think we already know."[4] Just as Simon had his view of the woman changed, will we see sinners as Jesus does? Just as the woman had her view of herself changed, will we see ourselves as God sees us? Just as the guests had their view of Jesus changed, will we see Jesus as he intends us to see him? When preaching a parable, allow for the spiritual reality that while your listeners will all hear the same thing, the Holy Spirit might apply it to different people in different ways. "*In preaching parables we grant ample room for listeners to react, think, and wonder, to draw connections and conclusions of their own.* A parable places great responsibility on its hearers. It does not tell us what it means but pushes us to consider what it means."[5] As such, people might see their own situation in the biblical text and be heartened that Scripture offers points of connections to their life. In other ways, the view through the window of the parable might present the need to see their life with God differently. Similarly, the window of the parable might show us how God sees others. Such a vision could call for uncomfortable yet necessary changes in our attitudes towards them.

When the parable becomes a window, the view may differ from one person to another, from one group to another. Our sermons need to have the wisdom to help such spiritual experiences.

Three diverse groups of students from Tanzania, Russia, and North America were invited to listen to the parable of the prodigal son (Luke 15:11-32) and then retell it in their own words..[6] As they retold the story, each group offered

---

4. McKenna, *Parables*, 102.
5. Duke, *Parables*, 99; emphasis in the original.
6. Powell, *What Do They Hear?*, 14–27.

different reasons as to why they thought the prodigal son ended up starving and being in need. The various reasons put forward by the groups were faithful to the biblical text and provided a window into their own social settings.

The Tanzanians observed that the prodigal was starving because no one gave him anything to eat (15:16). They understood what it meant for someone to be in a foreign country as an immigrant, unfamiliar with the customs of that place, and having lost their money. This group explained:

> The father's house is the kingdom of God that Jesus keeps talking about, but the far country is a society without honor. Everyone who heard this parable would be shocked by his depiction of such a society, a country that would let a stranger go hungry and not give him anything to eat. . . . the scribes and Pharisees are like that.[7]

The Russians saw the prodigal's awful need as being caused by a famine (15:14). This group were residents of St. Petersburg, whose history was coloured by the effects of a terrible siege in World War II. Hundreds of thousands of people died of starvation during this two-and-a-half-year siege. The Russian students were asked why they focused on the famine – rather than wastefulness – as the reason for the prodigal being in need. Their reply was, "So what if he lost his inheritance? . . . That just means he would be poor like everyone else. Most people don't have an inheritance to lose. But when the famine came, *that* was a problem."[8]

In contrast, the Americans' reply to why the prodigal was starving and feeding pigs centred on the son wasting his money (15:13, 30). Of the one hundred American students, only six mentioned the famine, while all one hundred mentioned the money being wasted. Their answer was a window into American life and values. The question is, do each of the groups see what the other groups see? It is the role of the preacher to help them do just that.

In a similar exercise in New Zealand, theology students – including pastors – from diverse cultures led groups from among some of the many immigrant groups who have now made New Zealand their home.[9] The groups were as culturally diverse as the leaders and included recent immigrants from China, young adults from immigrant families from Hong Kong, women refugees from Myanmar, a Filipino group who were a minority congregation

---

7. Powell, 27.
8. Powell, 18; emphasis in the original.
9. Wieland, "Cultivating Attentiveness," 98–117.

of a large English-speaking church, Rarotongan immigrants who were mature adults, a Fijian group from an Anglican church, Indian and Sri Lankan adults who were part of a Tamil congregation, New Zealand-born Samoans, Ni-Vanuatu women who were in the country as seasonal workers, and a group of young professional workers who did not profess faith in Christ. These groups reflected on two biblical stories, one of which was the prodigal son.[10]

The group leaders were instructed to have the parable of the prodigal son read in whichever language the group was most comfortable with, invite comments and responses from group members, and then allow the conversation to develop with as little intervention as possible by the leader. The leader's main task was not to correct or guide the group but to hear what the group saw in the story. The vision through the window included the Filipinos identifying with the prodigal son and resonating with the situation of going to a distant country, losing the family's investment in them, and experiencing shame and unfulfilled hopes. One leader, a Fijian minister, reported that two of his groups were so shocked by the younger son asking for his inheritance – which they saw as a scandalous cultural violation – that they did not even want to continue with the exercise.

The leaders and group members reported new levels of understanding through this exercise of becoming aware of what others saw through the window of Scripture. This was especially true where the leader was of a different cultural or social background to group members. Such leaders commented that although they thought they knew the group members, when they heard what their group saw in the biblical text, they realized that their vision had been limited.

> As the students reported back, a common theme was the way that the Bible passages had engaged the readers emotionally, connecting very directly with the realities of their own lives and experiences. In some groups, significant hurts and shame were brought into the open, anger was expressed, attitudes and assumptions were exposed and challenged, hope was felt, and direction found. . . . their own lives were being interwoven with the biblical narratives, opening up the potential for interpreting their lives within the framework of God's purpose and activity that they discerned or assumed in their stories. For the [group

---

10. The other biblical story was Paul's conversion on the road to Damascus (Acts 9:1–18).

leaders] the immediacy of connection that their groups found with the text was striking.[11]

The results described above could just as easily be a summary of the effect of the parable of the two debtors on listeners today. People see their situation in the parable, they see God seeing them, and they see each other in new ways because of God's work. When people look through the window presented by Scripture and see their lives before God accurately described, they discover that this world does not have the final word about life. They discover that the biblical world offers a new and timeless way to view their life in Christ and with others.

The work of the preacher involves considering how those listening to the sermon might see different things through the window of the parable. "Different readings of the same parable may also occur at different points in one's individual lifetime."[12] Yet, it is not only what individuals see that is important but also what the church as a community sees through the window. In the two debtors, we saw that both indviduals and the community were confronted with a new vision. How do we attend to this in our preaching? There is no quick and easy way to achieve this. Such work needs to happen outside the pulpit, through relationships with those to whom you preach. In the telling of the story of the two debtors, the text seems to imply that the woman had previously encountered Jesus. Some Bible commentators suggest that her actions were in response to Jesus having already forgiven her sins in an earlier encounter and that her anointing of Jesus was the loving action of an already-forgiven person. So, when Jesus said to her, "Your sins are forgiven," those words were as much for Simon and his guests to hear as for the woman. She already knew she had been forgiven but her community did not. The vision through the window of this parable was as much for Simon and his guests as for the woman. She had already seen this vision but her community had not.

One study shows that trained pastors and preachers are more likely to focus on what the biblical authors meant and intended when they wrote the Scriptures. In contrast, those who are listening to the sermon are more likely to focus on what the biblical text says to them and how they are personally affected.[13] To put it another way, preachers are more likely to preach the *meaning* of a biblical text ("this is what it meant when it was first written"),

---

11. Wieland, "Cultivating Attentiveness," 115–16.
12. Zimmermann, *Puzzling the Parables*, 7.
13. Powell, *What Do They Hear?*, 75–97.

while those we preach to are more likely to be listening for the *message* of a biblical text ("this is what it says to us today").[14] But preachers need to attend to both meaning and message. When preaching a parable and directing listeners' view through the window of that parable, aim to proclaim the original meaning of the parable as well as its present-day message at both a personal and community level.

The view through the window of the two debtors consists of the message about the forgiveness of sin. The view is also of the one who has compassion on the sinner and the authority to grant such forgiveness, and the response of love to his extravagant forgiveness. This needs to be preached.

The view through the window of the two debtors also consists of a message that impacts different people in different ways. Simon sees a reversal of status. The woman's love of God is described as "great," while Simon's love is described as "little." The woman experiences restoration through being received and restored by God. The guests see Jesus in a new way and are left searching for what this new vision means. And you and your listeners, what do you see? This needs to be preached.

Summary

We have considered how a parable is a picture, which becomes a mirror, and then a window. Through the window of the two debtors, we have seen the vision as experienced by those present when Jesus first told this story. As preachers, we have also considered how different people will catch different visions through the same window. The task of the preacher is to work at helping people see what others see as directed by the message of Scripture and the work of the Spirit. Our task when preaching is to remain faithful to the biblical text, while being aware of the situations of our listeners and remaining open to the work of the Spirit who shows them things that we have missed. With reference to our chart (Figure 12), we look "*through* the Window" and receive "Vision."

---

14. Powell, 97.

When preaching a parable, look...			
at the Picture	*in* the Mirror	*through* the Window	*beyond* the Door
We see life	We see ourselves	We see God	We see others
Sight	Insight	Vision	Imagination
Information	Intimidation	Invitation	Incarnation
Somebody else	Me!	God and me	God, me, and others
I'm interested	I'm shattered	I'm challenged	I'm called
Knowledge	Conviction	Revelation	Response

(Figure 12)

During your sermon preparation, you might discover that one of the other descriptions under "*through* the Window" seems a better choice. For instance, "We see God" might be the best description if your sermon focuses on what the guests saw when Jesus forgave the woman's sin and you reflect on how that speaks to your church. Perhaps your sermon preparation suggests that "Invitation" is a better word since the view through the window reveals that the woman was not the only sinner present that day. Who else might need to hear Jesus's assurance of forgiveness spoken to them? "God and me," which sums up the encounter by showing us what being accepted by God looks like, might be the message that your people need to embrace. "I'm challenged" might be the best response if we, like Simon, harbour self-righteous or judgemental attitudes towards others. And "Revelation" might be the best description when, through your sermon preparation, you see the effect of this parable in your life and the life of your church.

We have looked at the picture, in the mirror, and through the window. Now, the parable of the two debtors becomes a door. Our final task is to see what lies beyond that door.

Worksheet for "Window"

Scan the QR Code for a worksheet to help you look through the window of the parable.

https://bit.ly/PtP-Window

7

Look *Beyond* the Door

Geoff New

We come now to the final step in the model, the door. We have arrived at the door having seen the two debtors change from a picture to a mirror to a window. As the parable has changed in appearance, our understanding of Jesus's words have – hopefully! – changed along with it. Simply put, as the parable has changed in the way we look at it, what has happened in our heart during our sermon preparation? What will happen when we preach the parable? The combined effect of the parable as picture, mirror, and window come together and empower us to look "*beyond* the Door." The last verse of the events in and around the two debtors position us to do so.

Luke 7:50

> ⁵⁰ Jesus said to the woman, "Your faith has saved you; go in peace."

Jesus's words to the woman were for her personally and also for all who have ears to hear. His declaration marks the closing of one chapter of her life ("your faith has saved you") and the opening of a new chapter ("go in peace"). Jesus's statement that her faith had saved her spoke to her restoration as a whole person to the whole community. Elsewhere in the Gospel of Luke, Jesus uttered such words after healing someone from a physical condition: the woman who had been suffering from a physical condition that led to bleeding for twelve years (Luke 8:48); the Samaritan leper, the only one of the ten lepers healed who returned to thank Jesus (Luke 17:19); and the blind man who received his sight on the road to Jericho (Luke 18:42). Whether Jesus had forgiven sin or worked a healing miracle, the words "your faith has saved you" or "your faith has healed you" signified that the change had been more than only spiritual or only physical. Not only had Jesus changed the person entirely, the community also faced change. They had a new person in their midst; would they continue Jesus's ministry towards that person? This is the type of challenge we wrestle with in this the last stage of responding to a parable – looking beyond the door. Our progress through the parable is depicted in our chart (Figure 13). We have looked at the picture and received "Sight," looked in the mirror and gained "Insight," and looked through the window and obtained "Vision." Now, at the door, we exercise "Imagination."

When preaching a parable, look . . .			
at the Picture	*in* the Mirror	*through* the Window	*beyond* the Door
Sight	Insight	Vision	Imagination

(Figure 13)

The questions and challenges raised by Jesus's ministry to the woman are as demanding today as when they were first raised in Simon's house. As we study and preach the two debtors, we now shift our gaze from the picture it presents, the mirror it holds up, and the window it throws open to the door to which it now leads. Beyond that door, our imagination of how to live with one another in community is defined by honouring what Christ has done.

> Luke closes the curtains on this scene before the action is completed. It is one thing to have Jesus proclaim her forgiveness in order that her renewed status might be recognized by the community; it is quite another for that community actually to accept his pronouncement and to extend kinship to her. How will they respond? Will they adopt the view of the world that Jesus displays in his interactions in this episode? Will they learn to view God as one who cancels debts and invites others to do the same so that all might behave toward one another with love . . . ? Will they recognize Jesus as God's authorized agent to pronounce forgiveness and to bring restoration? How will they respond? How will Simon respond? And how will Luke's readers respond?[1]

Beyond the door, the woman stands for what Jesus can do in a person's life and represents Jesus's presence in a community. In the NT, one thing is clear: Jesus made people ambassadors. Jesus equates our treatment of others with

---

1. Green, *Luke*, 314–15.

our treatment of him. He takes our behaviour towards others personally. We see this in the parable of the sheep and the goats (Matt 25:31–46). We see this in the way the ascended Christ spoke to Saul on the road to Damascus: "Saul, Saul, why do you persecute me? . . . I am Jesus, whom you are persecuting" (Acts 9:4–5). The woman of Luke 7 models how we ought to respond to God's forgiveness and fuels our imagination about life in the future.

> Having received forgiveness, we should go into the world in peace, just as Jesus told the woman to do: "Your faith has saved you; go in peace" (7:50). To "go in peace" means to go into the world forgiving others just as we have been forgiven. The gospel of peace has revolutionary consequences spiritually and socially, in the here and now.[2]

In our sermon, all our insights and study lead to this place of preaching the parable as a door. This part of our sermon is vital because, as we stand at the door – filled with the content we have received from the picture-mirror-window – we are confronted with a question: "Do we mean it?" All that we have learned and wrestled with as the parable changed from picture to mirror to window is useless if we now turn away from the door. "The parables compel us – for Christ's sake literally – to do something!"[3] Our response to the parable up to this point in our sermon is now put to the test: Do we mean it?

One further point needs to be made about doors. In the NT, when a door is used as an image of God's call or a ministry opportunity, evil is often at work, causing difficulties and trying to frustrate the kingdom's advance. For instance, Paul writes that "a great door for effective work has opened to me, and there are many who oppose me" (1 Cor 16:9). On another occasion, although Paul entered a door opened by the Lord, he "still had no peace of mind" (2 Cor 2:12–13). In Colossians 4:3, Paul, while praying for an open door, reminded the Colossians that he was in chains. Jesus placed an open door before the church of Philadelphia but acknowledged that they had little strength and had experienced hardship from those who were from the "synagogue of Satan" (Rev 3:8–9). When you come to the stage of preaching the parable as a door, be mindful that as you and your people seek to obey the word of God, you may also experience spiritual struggles.

When preaching parables, preachers often retell the parable using situations and characters drawn from present-day life in an attempt to make

---

2. Takatemjen, "Luke," 1350.
3. Snodgrass, *Stories with Intent*, 9.

the parable understandable and accessible for today's listeners. However, this exercise can still sometimes result in our hearers holding the parable at a safe distance. A more penetrating exercise, that will help your listeners see beyond the door, is to retell the setting in which the parable was first spoken. In your sermon, retell the setting as if the events surrounding the parable happened in your church or wider community; then drop the parable into your setting without changing the parable itself. Remember, your listeners would have been informed about the parable from what you preached about the parable as a picture.[4] For instance, you could describe the situation that led to the telling of the two debtors like this:

> One of the leaders of our church invited a guest preacher to lunch after the Sunday morning worship service. Attendance at the lunch was by invitation only, and there were about twenty people present. The food was laid out on the table, and people began helping themselves. They each took a plate, filled it with food, and found a seat. The guest preacher, however, stood back, allowing others to get their food first. When everyone had served their lunch, sat down, and begun eating, he approached the table. However, not only were there no plates left, there was also hardly any food left. If anyone had looked up from their meal, they would have noticed that the guest preacher looked embarrassed. He took a couple of small scraps of food in his hand and turned to find a seat. But there were no seats left. He retreated to the edge of the room and leaned against the wall, eating his scraps of food.
>
> A woman who had not been invited was also present at the lunch. She had attended the church for many years but had left several months earlier. No one had been sorry to see her leave the church. She was known by everyone because they had all been the target of her habit of gossiping. That morning, she had turned up unexpectedly to the worship service. During the sermon on James 3:3–12 – about the power of the tongue – she had been seen weeping. Perhaps her tears were in response to the preaching, but most people thought that unlikely. Because of the way she spoke about others, she had a reputation of being a cold and cruel woman. She had been that way for years, and no one

---

4. See chapter 3: "Look *at* the Picture."

believed that her heart would be open to the word of God in any meaningful way.

While the rest were eating their lunch, this woman approached the preacher. She took him by the hand and guided him to the seat she had been occupying. When he was seated, she gave him her plate of food, which she had not yet begun to eat. Her voice cracked with emotion as she fought back her tears. She thanked him for his sermon, saying that his words had touched her deeply. She then went to the edge of the room and stood where the preacher had been standing earlier on.

The church leader was angry. He thought to himself, "The preacher has no idea what kind of person she is! He thinks she treats everyone that way and is open to God. If only he knew what we all know!"

Imagine that, after telling a story like this in your sermon, you read aloud the two debtors as it appears in Luke 7 and then ask Jesus's question of your listeners: "Now which of them will love him more?" (7:42). Next, you apply the parable to your church by contrasting the gossiping woman's kindness towards the preacher in contrast to the others' lack of attention to him. You quote Jesus as saying that her many sins have been forgiven (7:47). Then, to add to the impact and help your people see beyond the door, you say something like this:

> And so, Jesus announces to such a person in our church, "Your faith has saved you; go in peace." Jesus announces it to her, and he announces it to us. Here are the questions that now confront us: "Can we accept Jesus's pronouncement, made in our hearing, to her? Can we now live with her – and anyone else like her – as a sister in Christ?"

To draw on the description from Figure 13, seeing *"beyond* the Door" requires us to exercise our "Imagination." To make the message of this parable true among us, what needs to change within our hearts, in our behaviour, in our relationships with one another, and in our understanding of God?

This part of our sermon requires courage and integrity. We need the courage to say true yet difficult things about our community life. We also need to recognize that, as preachers, we must examine our own response to the parable so that we can preach it with integrity.

There is one more thing to keep in mind when you look beyond the door that the parable opens. Parables have two things in common with OT stories.

First, people can be overfamiliar with them. They have heard the story before, and they know how it ends. Second, things are never what they seem to be. "It is in the nature of parable to be unpredictable."[5] So, we must preach the plain meaning of Scripture *and* also mine the text for deeper meaning.

These two concerns can be likened to something that one of our authors (Geoff New) often noted when in India. He would approach a door to some place and that door would frequently be old, crumbling, and ordinary. With its broken-down in appearance, there was nothing inviting about the door. Beyond that door, however, there would often be utter beauty and wonder. The door might lead to a shop full of colourful and stunning cloth. Or beyond the door might lie peaceful accommodation, overlooking a lake and surrounded by hills and trees. The effect of these experiences on the author was that, thereafter, no matter how common a door looked, he was now full of expectation as he wondered what surprise lay beyond it. So it is with the door of parables. People can be overfamiliar with these stories. The parable may appear to them as old and ordinary. However, things are never what they seem. Beyond the door lies beauty and wonder. Your task as a preacher is to open that door so that people can walk into the wonders of God. But how do we do that?

As with an OT story, the way to combat people's familiarity and help them to discover that things are never what they seem is to revisit the start of the story. Surprisingly, while people are usually familiar with how a Bible story ends, they are not always familiar with how it begins. The beginning of the story describes the situation or problem. By revisiting the beginning of the story, you can deepen the meaning by dwelling in the opening situation and any problem that the characters of the story are confronted with. With the two debtors, the story is brief. You might think that there is not much to say about the beginning. Yet, pause and think a little longer. "Two people owed money to a certain money-lender. One owed him five hundred denarii, and the other fifty" (7:41). You could dwell on the way the story is worded. The emphasis is on those in debt rather than on the money-lender who was simply going about his normal business. Personal information is laid bare. The size of each person's debt is revealed. How would it be if we all knew how much money each of us owed? How would you feel? Embarrassed? Humiliated? One of the debtors owes ten times the amount owed by the other. Does the one owing more feel jealousy or resentment towards the other who did not need to secure such a big loan?

---

5. Duke, *Parables*, 7.

In your preaching, as you seek to direct people's gaze beyond the door, reminding them about the start of the parable can result in a stark contrast between the before and after of the story. You could also highlight what was and what can be. We are looking beyond the door with "Imagination" (Figure 13). By acknowledging that our listeners might be overfamiliar with the two debtors and that things are never what they seem, reaching back to the start of the parable could remind them of who they are and point them through the door to who Christ is creating them to be.

Summary

As we reach the door – the final stage of the parable – we look beyond it with "Imagination." When Jesus first told this parable of the two debtors, he seemed to have focused on two people but, later, everyone present was swept up by its grace and truth. As with the earlier stages of the parable, our chart supplies a range of different descriptions of how parables can speak to us.

When preaching a parable, look . . .			
at the Picture	*in* the Mirror	*through* the Window	*beyond* the Door
We see life	We see ourselves	We see God	We see others
Sight	Insight	Vision	Imagination
Information	Intimidation	Invitation	Incarnation
Somebody else	Me!	God and me	God, me, and others
I'm interested	I'm shattered	I'm challenged	I'm called
Knowledge	Conviction	Revelation	Response

(Figure 14)

We have stayed with "Imagination," but your study might well have led you to cry, "We see others." Alternatively, through the Spirit working in your heart and mind, your sermon at this point might be best served by using the word "Incarnation." Your sermon has developed so that you find you must preach about what it means for you as a church to dwell among others in the Spirit of Christ. As your sermon reaches this last stage, you may discover that "God, me, and others" is the most fitting description and feel compelled to speak about how each of these lie beyond the door, both separately and together. Perhaps, as you look beyond the door, you see something for the first time and discern God's voice and conclude, "I'm called." Maybe at this point your sermon centres on the word "Response," and you offer the opportunity for people to respond by challenging them with an action that goes beyond words and extends to serving in practical ways.

The last stage of the parable, the door, can be unpredictable and wild.

> It is as if a parable were a journey on which Jesus is our guide. He takes us through landscapes that we know. We recognize this feature and that, and relax into comfort. Then, abruptly, the scenery turns strange . . . The inhabitants become bizarre. Suddenly, Jesus disappears; the tour is over. Looking around us, we see we have arrived at nothing that looks like a destination; it is more like a crossroads. Where we go from here is a puzzle left for us to discern.[6]

The parable leads us to the door where we can continue to surrender our lives into God's hands, saying, "Yes Lord – your kingdom come, your will be done, on earth as it is in heaven."

Worksheet for "Door"

Scan the QR Code for a worksheet to help you look beyond the door of the parable.

https://bit.ly/PtP-Door

---

6. Duke, 11.

Part 2

Now, having explained the Picture-Mirror-Window-Door model of interpreting parables in these chapters, we look at how this works out in practice in the following chapter by means of example sermons.

8

The Parable of Three Men and a Lamb (2 Samuel 12:1–13)

Paul Windsor

Creating the Sermon Using the Picture-Mirror-Window-Door Model

Our first sermon engages with 2 Samuel 12:1–13. This sermon shows how the Picture-Mirror-Window-Door model can be used to track the movement in the story of David, Nathan, and the parable told by Nathan. For this sermon, the main headings employ the language of Picture-Mirror-Window-Door rather than the more detailed descriptions under each column in Figure 15.

When preaching a parable, look . . .			
at the Picture	*in* the Mirror	*through* the Window	*beyond* the Door
We see life	We see ourselves	We see God	We see others
Sight	Insight	Vision	Imagination
Information	Intimidation	Invitation	Incarnation
Somebody else	Me!	God and I	God, I, and others
I'm interested	I'm shattered	I'm challenged	I'm called
Knowledge	Conviction	Revelation	Response

(Figure 15)

The Sermon
2 Samuel 12:1–13

The Lord sent Nathan to David. When he came to him, he said, "There were two men in a certain town, one rich and the other poor. ² The rich man had a very large number of sheep and cattle, ³ but the poor man had nothing except one little ewe lamb that he had bought. He raised it, and it grew up with him and his children. It shared his food, drank from his cup and even slept in his arms. It was like a daughter to him.

⁴ "Now a traveller came to the rich man, but the rich man refrained from taking one of his own sheep or cattle to prepare a meal for the traveller who had come to him. Instead, he took the ewe lamb that belonged to the poor man and prepared it for the one who had come to him."

⁵ David burned with anger against the man and said to Nathan, "As surely as the Lord lives, the man who did this must die! ⁶ He must pay for that lamb four times over, because he did such a thing and had no pity."

⁷ Then Nathan said to David, "You are the man! This is what the Lord, the God of Israel, says: 'I anointed you king over Israel, and I delivered you from the hand of Saul. ⁸ I gave your master's house to you, and your master's wives into your arms. I gave you all Israel and Judah. And if all this had been too little, I would have given you even more. ⁹ Why did you despise the word of the Lord by doing what is evil in his eyes? You struck down Uriah the Hittite with the sword and took his wife to be your own. You killed him with the sword of the Ammonites. ¹⁰ Now, therefore, the sword shall never depart from your house, because you despised me and took the wife of Uriah the Hittite to be your own.'

¹¹ "This is what the Lord says: 'Out of your own household I am going to bring calamity on you. Before your very eyes I will take your wives and give them to one who is close to you, and he will sleep with your wives in broad daylight. ¹² You did it in secret, but I will do this thing in broad daylight before all Israel.'"

¹³ Then David said to Nathan, "I have sinned against the Lord."

Nathan replied, "The Lord has taken away your sin. You are not going to die."

A Picture from Nathan (12:1–4)

In 2 Samuel 11:27, we read that "the thing David had done displeased the Lord." This leads to Nathan paying King David a visit. No drama. No shouting. No condemnation. Nathan simply paints a picture, with its own caption: Three Men and a Lamb. Let me introduce each one to you.

There is a "rich man," described quickly with one phrase – "he had a very large number of sheep and cattle" – that defines him in terms of his possessions. There is a "poor man," described slowly, with four phrases. We linger with him in his home, with his family. It is very tender. There is a "travelling man," and so hospitality is expected. The rich man must open his own home and prepare a meal for the traveller.

There is "a lamb." It was little. It had been purchased and then raised in the family of the poor man. It shared the poor man's food, drank from his cup, and slept in his bed. "It was like a daughter to him." And yet, the rich man, who owned flocks and herds beyond what could be numbered or named, chooses to *take* this lamb – beloved, numbered, and (probably) named – to make the meal for his guest. He was so cruel. "He took what was not his and treated it as if it were his own."[1]

This is the picture from Nathan. When first written it was a story of sixty-one words, a work of pure fiction but so realistic in its detail that David the *shepherd* is pulled into it. He can see it happening. He knows the characters. He catches the nuances. And if the realism in the picture pulls in David the *shepherd*, then the injustice in it ignites David the *king*, who also doubles as the *judge*. David is outraged. Correct the wrong. Hand out some punishment. Pass a sentence . . . and he does, right there and then. The rich man deserves to die – even though he hadn't killed anyone. "He must pay for that lamb four times over." There he is – King David – so full of compassion, with such a strong, clear sense of right and wrong.

Yet, there is more in the passage. Nathan is up to something. In speaking truth to power, he is taking some risks. Nathan uses a story rather than a sermon or even an oracle. He chooses to be short, simple – and subversive. He slips under the defences of the king by being disarming and indirect. He is trying to trap David, to corner him. Unknown to Nathan or David, the narrator helps us see the trap being set. The picture is painted with some of the

---

1. Brueggemann, *First and Second Samuel*, 280.

same words from chapter 11. The rich man *takes* the lamb in chapter 12 just as David took Bathsheba in chapter 11. The "eat, drink, lie" (2 Sam 12:3) that the lamb does with the poor man is what Uriah refused to do with his wife, Bathsheba, when David sent for him (2 Sam 11:11). Some even see a similarity in the words used for lamb and for Bathsheba.

This is the sort of artistry for which the OT is famous. Nathan is laying a trap, and the narrator helps us to see it being set. In his rage and righteousness, David walks right into the trap.

At just the right moment, Nathan delivers the punchline – which, in his language, is just two words. As a hush falls over the scene, the picture becomes a mirror.

A Mirror for David (12:6a)

"You are the man!" In that moment, David is exposed. He had identified with the poor man but now discovers that he is the rich man. In pointing one angry finger, he realizes that three other fingers are pointing back at himself.

Some persistent sinful human nature is on display here. In recent years, there have been many scandals among Christian leaders – proclaimed by big, loud, public headlines. And those who condemn the scandals the loudest can often see in the mirror their own scandal – small, quiet, private, and hidden from view. When I was a student at seminary, one of my professors reminded us, "When you point out the sins of others keep an eye on the other fingers pointing back. Does your heated righteousness betray your own battle? If so, deal with it. Don't project it." Part of David's outrage is fuelled by an unease deep within his own soul. His anger is fuelled not just by the injustice he saw but by the guilt he felt.

In that moment when Nathan's picture becomes David's mirror, David sees himself in a new light. He feels the weight of his own crimes. After all, he has been flouting commandments right, left and centre, coveting, comitting adultery, and even murder, breaking the tenth, seventh, and sixth commandments. But the Lord was watching, and now, Nathan – putting on the mantle of the prophet and sounding like a Micah or an Amos – directly and boldly confronts David.

Once again – for us, if not for David – the narrator helps us see this confrontation. The artistry continues. In all his sinning, David is the orchestrator of the action. Twelve times, in chapter 11, David is portrayed as doing the "sending." Joab is sent. Messengers are sent to get Bathsheba. Uriah is sent for. A gift is sent. It goes on and on. David has the power. But how does chapter 12 begin? "The LORD sent Nathan to David" (12:1). Just when David thinks he has got away with his "sendings," God does a sending of his own. The word "send" seems to hold this entire section together. This is a story about power – its abuse by David and its right and proper use by God.

As we've been chatting here, our gaze has already begun moving to the next view.

A Window on God (12:6b–12)

God is in control. He is at the centre of the story. David missed this fact. It is easy to do. It happens again and again in the training of preachers. Open up a story in the Old Testament. Ask people, "OK, *who* is in this story, and what can you observe about them?" Often, God is the last character mentioned. People just do not see him in the story. Far from being in control, God may even seem invisible.

As we try to identify this window on God, let's look for God as we read.

"The thing David had done displeased the LORD" (11:27).

"The LORD sent Nathan to David" (12:1).

"This is what the LORD, the God of Israel, says: 'I anointed you . . . I delivered you'" (12:7).

"I gave you all Israel . . . and if all this had been too little, I would have given you even more" (12:8).

"Why did you despise the word of the LORD by doing what is evil in his eyes?" (12:9). "You despised me" (12:10).

"I am going to bring calamity on you. Before your very eyes, I will take your wives and give them to one who is close to you . . . You did it in secret, but I will do this thing in broad daylight" (12:11-12).

On and on it goes. The hand of God is behind it all. And it is not just God's sovereignty and control that we see through this window. We also see God's grace in all that he has given David and in his willingness to give even more. Even sending Nathan was an act of grace, to save David from himself. We also see God's justice in the indictment (12:9), which is followed by a sentence (12:10-12) – a sentence that shapes and directs the rest of 2 Samuel.

And yet, so much is left unsaid, isn't it? Especially around victims like Bathsheba, who was so abused and who lost so much. However, in his grace and justice, God orchestrates events so that Bathsheba would receive a mention in the genealogy of the Saviour, Jesus, where she appears as Uriah's wife (Matt 1:6). So it is God, in all the fullness of his character, who takes this story forward. He is sovereign. He is gracious. He is just.

This brings us back to David and his final look in the mirror: "Then David said to Nathan, 'I have sinned against the LORD'" (12:13). Yes, David had sinned against Bathsheba and against Uriah, but the cause of those sins, the root of it all, was something deeper. He had rebelled against God, displeasing him and despising his word. Once again, this is expressed in just two words in the language of the day: "You are the man." To which David responds, "I have sinned against the LORD." Brief. Immediate. Blunt. No excuses. No projections. David has a broken spirit and acknowledges his sin. As Eugene Peterson comments, "Our primary task isn't to avoid sin, which is impossible anyway, but to recognise it."[2]

In that moment, David walks towards a door – and a future.

A Door for David (12:13)

There is a way forward for David. As he repents – of coveting, adultery, murder, and abuse of power – there is forgiveness: "The LORD has taken away your sin. You are not going to die" (12:13). Whether or not our sins are of the same magnitude as David's, James makes it clear that each one of us faces a similar battle to David: "Each person is tempted when they are dragged away by their own evil desire and enticed. Then, after desire has conceived, it gives birth to sin; and sin, when it is full-grown, gives birth to death" (Jas 1:14–15).

This is what people in a previous century referred to as "the exceeding sinfulness of sin."[3] Whether it is David's headline scandals or our own private scandals, if sin is not viewed as exceedingly bad, everything collapses. Grace is cheapened, forgiveness is flicked aside, and the whole transforming dynamic of the gospel crumbles. Our lives, if not our mouths, sing, "innocuous grace, how dull the sound that saved a nice person like me!"

A woman who had lived a sinful life and knew it once rushed into the home of Simon the Pharisee, a respected religious leader (Luke 7:36–50). Jesus

---

2. Peterson, *Leap Over a Wall*, 186.
3. From the title of a book by English Puritan Jeremiah Burroughs (1599–1646).

was there. She fell at Jesus's feet. She wet his feet with her tears. She wiped his feet with her hair and poured exquisite perfume over them. And, like David, Simon explodes. He is outraged. This time, it is Jesus who lays the trap with a picture that becomes a mirror, then a window, and, finally, the offer of a door. Simon doesn't seem to make it to the door. What a shame! But the woman does! "Your sins are forgiven." Her exceeding sinfulness is forgiven, and she heads for the door and a fresh future with Jesus's words ringing in her ears: "The one who is forgiven much, loves much; the one who is forgiven little, loves little" (Luke 7:47).

Today, our world needs people who love much because they know they've been forgiven much. These are the people God uses to change the world. These are the ones who sing, truly and deeply, with both their life and their mouth, "Amazing grace, how sweet the sound that saved a wretch like me."

Observation and Discussion

Jesus did not invent the parable. It is a literary form or genre that already existed and which the writers of the OT also used. Our first sermon provides us with an example of the Picture-Mirror-Window-Door model at work in the OT – even using the terms picture, mirror, window, and door to give shape to the sermon.

1. Notice how, right through the sermon, Paul Windsor takes care to observe the details in both this text and in the wider context. What are some of those details?

2. What methods does he use to make the Picture section vivid for us?

3. In the Mirror section, Paul Windsor refers to a story from his time at seminary. How does this story illustrate what King David saw in the mirror? And how does this model how we might look in the mirror?

4. As humans, our eyes are naturally drawn to the people who are like us in the biblical story. But the Window section forces us to look for God – who he is and what he is doing. What do we learn about God in this story?

5. Notice how a gospel story is used in the Door section without doing violence to the OT text. The purpose of using a gospel story in this way is to confront us with the force of the story about King David. We hear the words "You are the woman" or "You are the man" as we walk through the door into new spaces with the Spirit.

9

The Workers in the Vineyard (Matthew 20:1–16)

Geoff New

Creating the Sermon Using the Picture-Mirror-Window-Door Model

After carefully studying Matthew 20:1–16, while bearing in mind the skills for interpreting parables that were discussed in chapter 2, a sermon structure can be created. In the chart (Figure 16), the descriptions which best show the parable moving through the stages of Picture-Mirror-Window-Door are selected. The choices made for this sermon are shown below:

When preaching a parable, look . . .			
at the Picture	*in* the Mirror	*through* the Window	*beyond* the Door
We see life	We see ourselves	We see God	We see others
Sight	Insight	Vision	Imagination
Information	Intimidation	Invitation	Incarnation
Somebody else	Me!	God and me	God, me, and others
I'm interested	I'm shattered	I'm challenged	I'm called
Knowledge	Conviction	Revelation	Response

(Figure 16)

The Sermon
Matthew 20:1–16

"For the kingdom of heaven is like a landowner who went out early in the morning to hire workers for his vineyard. ² He agreed to pay them a denarius for the day and sent them into his vineyard.

³ "About nine in the morning he went out and saw others standing in the market-place doing nothing. ⁴ He told them, 'You also go and work in my vineyard, and I will pay you whatever is right.' ⁵ So they went.

"He went out again about noon and about three in the afternoon and did the same thing. ⁶ About five in the afternoon he went out and found still others standing around. He asked them, 'Why have you been standing here all day long doing nothing?'

⁷ "'Because no one has hired us,' they answered.

"He said to them, 'You also go and work in my vineyard.'

⁸ "When evening came, the owner of the vineyard said to his foreman, 'Call the workers and pay them their wages, beginning with the last ones hired and going on to the first.'

⁹ "The workers who were hired about five in the afternoon came and each received a denarius. ¹⁰ So when those came who were hired first, they expected to receive more. But each one of them also received a denarius. ¹¹ When they received it, they began to grumble against the landowner. ¹² 'These who were hired last worked only one hour,' they said, 'and you have made them equal to us who have borne the burden of the work and the heat of the day.'

¹³ "But he answered one of them, 'I am not being unfair to you, friend. Didn't you agree to work for a denarius? ¹⁴ Take your pay and go. I want to give the one who was hired last the same as I gave you. ¹⁵ Don't I have the right to do what I want with my own money? Or are you envious because I am generous?'

¹⁶ "So the last will be first, and the first will be last."

Picture: I'm Interested

The opening scenes of this parable are marked by a sense of urgency on the part of the landowner and increasing desperation on the part of the workers.

"I'm interested" – what events might have led to such urgency and desperation?

The time of the year is late spring, which is harvest time. The landowner needs to get his crop of grapes harvested before they spoil on the vine. His urgency is seen in the fact that he visits the market-place five times on the same day to hire labourers. We don't know why he kept returning for more workers. Did he underestimate how many he needed at the start of the day? Were the first workers slow, making it necessary to find more workers to complete the work? Were there not enough workers for hire in the market-place when he first went there? Whatever the reason, the landowner's urgency is seen in his repeated trips to the market-place.

We sense the desperation on the part of the workers. These workers were, in some ways, worse off than slaves. They were day labourers, earning a basic daily wage of one denarius. At that time in Palestine, the basic cost of living for an adult was half a denarius a day. Unlike slaves, whose basic needs were provided for by their masters, day labourers – who were sometimes exploited and often unemployed – could not always meet their basic needs. So, harvest time brought hope of work but also a flood of workers competing for work. Each day, desperate labourers populated the market-place.

In Matthew 20:1–7, the urgency of the landowner and the desperation of the workers meet. The working day dawns. Rabbis defined the working day in this way: "Working hours last from the dawning of the sun to the rising of the stars."[1] What would this day hold for the landowner and for the labourers? The landowner's first recruitment takes place around 6:00 a.m., and he agrees to pay the going rate of one denarius (20:1–2). At 9:00 a.m., he employs the next group of workers, with the promise to pay "whatever is right" (20:4). While no speech is recorded at noon and 3:00 p.m., we are told that he did the same thing (20:5). At 5:00 p.m. – with one hour left in the workday – the landowner makes his final trip to the market-place (20:6–7). Here we read the longest conversation in the parable, with the landowner asking the workers why they have been "standing here all day long doing nothing" (20:6). Of all the groups hired, theirs is the only response that is recorded: "Because no one has hired

---

1. Schweizer, *Matthew*, 392.

us" (20:7). Was it their fault? Did they arrive late to the market-place? Did no one hire them because they were bad workers? These questions remain unanswered. The landowner does not challenge the response given by this last group of workers. But of all the groups, theirs is the only one who are not given any idea what they will earn. They are simply told, "You also go and work in my vineyard" (20:7). Only the first group is told they will earn a denarius; everyone else is left with the reasonable expectation they will be paid less in keeping with their reduced hours of work.

The first hearers of this parable would have assumed the same outcome if they had been in that situation; they would receive pay in line with how many hours they worked. As we hear the parable and picture these first-century events unfolding, we respond to the Spirit, who brings Jesus's story to bear on our lives, by saying, "I'm interested."

So, the first part of the parable comes to a resting place. The urgent landowner managed to employ the workers he needed, and the desperate day labourers received at least some work that day. All seems well. Crisis avoided.

Mirror: Me!

If a sense of urgency and desperation marks the first part of the story, anger marks the next part. When evening comes, the vineyard owner directs his supervisor to pay the workers (20:8). All would have been well if the owner had simply instructed the supervisor to "call the workers and pay them their wages" and said nothing else. However, he doesn't stop there but adds, "beginning with the last ones hired and going on to the first" (20:8). Since all the workers are present when the one-hour workers are paid, they see these latecomers receiving  a full day's wage for doing a fraction of the work. While this is a surprise to the first group of workers, surely it is good news? If the one-hour workers received a denarius, that must mean that a denarius is the hourly rate and not a daily rate, right?! Today is a good day! They can afford to sleep in tomorrow and even take a few days off work. Then comes their turn to receive their pay and, understandably, "they expected to receive more" (20:10). They are stunned when they receive the same amount as the latecomers. This must be a mistake! Surprise turns to shock. Excited expectation gives way to outrage. They are angry. They grumble against the landowner, and their cold anger is also directed against the 5:00 p.m. workers. They hold their fellow workers in contempt because these labourers have been made "equal to us who have borne the burden of the work and the heat of the day" (20:12).

The accusation "You have made them equal to us" exposes the heart of those who spoke those words. These words expose "Me!" John the Baptist described his ambition with these words: "He [Jesus] must become greater; I must become less" (John 3:30). This parable describes a different ambition: "I must remain greater; they must remain less." Here, the parable describes "Me!" We hear echoes of Jonah's fury towards God for showing mercy to Nineveh: "But to Jonah this seemed very wrong, and he became angry . . . 'Now, Lord, take away my life, for it is better for me to die than to live'" (Jonah 4:1, 4). We hear the same bitter spirit in the words of the elder brother in the parable of the prodigal son: "Look! All these years I've been slaving for you and never disobeyed your orders. Yet you never gave me even a young goat so I could celebrate with my friends" (Luke 15:29). Echoed here are Peter's words, shortly after the resurrected Jesus commissioned him, when Peter compared his call with John's: "Lord, what about him?" (John 21:21). I am reminded of the words of a Christian sister after I had conducted the funeral of someone who had received Christ on their deathbed. She said, "I wish I could live a life of sin and wait until the last moment to come into the kingdom." Here we see the sin of looking sideways towards others with anger or envy instead of looking upwards to God with gratitude and humility.

Here I see "Me!"

In response to the group of angry workers, the landowner answers only one of them (20:13). Perhaps this man was the ringleader. That only one from the group is singled out opens us up to the possibility that we, too, need a one-to-one conversation about our attitude. The landowner says to the one – and God says to us – "I am not being unfair to you, friend" (20:13). Matthew is the only gospel writer to use this address "friend." He uses this term three times in his gospel, each time signalling that something is not right in a relationship. We see this most dramatically when, after Judas betrayed Jesus with a kiss, Jesus said to him, "Do what you came for, friend" (Matt 26:50). The use of the title "friend" in Matthew's gospel signals God's abundant love and our lack of love. The use of the title "friend" signals God's faithfulness in the presence of our unfaithfulness.

Does God call you "friend" to alert you to his love towards you or to highlight your anger towards him or others? In your pursuit of and service in the kingdom and its righteousness, do you harbour a sense that you have been treated unfairly? Consider your answers carefully. Answer slowly. The true state of your heart is found in your level of agreement with the twelve-hour workers' complaint and what you believe you deserve but have not received. Your true answer is found in the complaints you make to others rather than in what you say to God in prayer. To put it another way, your true answer is the sense of injustice you harbour in your heart about how God treats the "undeserving" rather than what you say to God.

One Bible commentator writes about this parable, "Those who had worked all day lost nothing; justice was served, but mercy was added."[2] God is not being unfair to you, friend. Do you believe that? A secret lurks in the human heart; we can be inclined to have no problem with God gifting grace to people, but only if they receive something of what their sin deserves first. The parable of the workers in the vineyard places us before God and tests our hearts as justice, mercy, and grace are gifted to others. This story places us before God with the uncomfortable reminder of the temptation we all fight against – and have done so since the serpent first uttered the lie in the garden of Eden – to "be like God" (Gen 3:5). The workers in the vineyard exposes our arrogance in demanding an explanation from God about how he manages his vineyard. The parable reveals whether we presume to make judgements about God's grace. The workers in the vineyard exposes our sin by having us state what *we* would do if we owned the vineyard. To all this, God simply says, "I am not being unfair to you, friend."

And in this, "We see God"!

Window: We See God

Matthew 20:13–15 describes the landowner's response to the anger of the workers. The landowner responds with a series of statements and questions.

> "Didn't you agree to work for a denarius? Take your pay and go. I want to give the one who was hired last the same as I gave you. Don't I have the right to do what I want with my own money? Or are you envious because I am generous?" (Matt 20:13–15)

Consider how we see God in each of these statements and questions. "I want to give . . . Don't I have the right to do what I want . . . Or are you envious because I am generous?"

---

2. Keener, *Matthew*, 483.

"I want to give" – we see the grace of God.

"Don't I have the right to do what I want?" – we see the sovereignty of God.

"Or are you envious because I am generous?" – we see the goodness of God.

These statements and questions all began with the searching question, "Didn't you agree . . . ?" (20:13). The day had begun with the workers responding positively to the landowner, and all seemed good, right, and fair. They knew what they were agreeing to, and they had received what had been promised. This all began with us responding to the invitation and call of God to serve and love him. And all seemed good, right, and fair. We knew what we were agreeing to, and we thought we knew God. Yet, the Lord is "the compassionate and gracious God, slow to anger, abounding in love and faithfulness" (Exod 34:6). We can never plumb the depths of his character and "out of his fullness we have all received grace in place of grace already given" (John 1:16). His generosity overwhelms, and while we gladly receive it for ourselves, we may find God's generosity offensive when we see others – who, by our standards, are undeserving – being blessed. In such moments, can you see God as he is portrayed in this parable?

In the parable, the landowner asks the question, "Are you envious because I am generous?" The question has the sense, "Do you have an evil eye because I am good?" This is confronting.

Can we see God?

If our vision clears, we will see a gracious, sovereign, and good God. If our eye is evil, we will be blinded by envy because this vision of God is unfair by our reckoning. Indeed, the God described in this parable seems reckless. We can imagine the risk the landowner takes. What will happen the next day when he goes to the market-place to hire workers? Who would want to work for him all day when they could get paid the same rate for just one hour? What if you were one of the workers who showed up at the market-place the next day at 6:00 a.m. and he offered you work? Would you accept or decline? The landowner now has a reputation. God has an even more outrageous reputation. Do you see God as revealed in this parable? Will you work for such a gracious, sovereign, and good God even when you do not think he has treated you fairly?

Elie Wiesel – a Holocaust survivor and winner of the 1986 Nobel Peace Prize – described an experience he had as a fifteen-year-old boy in Auschwitz. A rabbi took him to a barracks to watch three scholarly rabbis place God on trial for crimes against creation and humanity. If ever a group of God's people had cause to wonder about whether God was indeed just and merciful, it is those who suffered at that time in history. Over a period of three nights, the rabbis called witnesses and gathered evidence. They then reached their verdict:

the Lord God Almighty, Creator of heaven and earth, was guilty as charged. Wiesel records that after the verdict was announced, there was an "infinity of silence."[3] Then one of the rabbis broke the silence: "It is time for evening prayer."[4] And so, they prayed and worshipped the God they felt aggrieved by.

They still saw God.

Door: God, Me, and Others

The story immediately before this parable is the story of Jesus's encounter with the rich young man (Matt 19:16–22). The disciples are astonished by Jesus's comments about this encounter and about the difficulty the rich have in entering the kingdom of heaven (19:23–25). Jesus then promises that those who have sacrificed to follow him "will receive a hundred times as much and will inherit eternal life" (19:29) and concludes by saying, "But many who are first will be last, and many who are last will be first" (19:30). He then tells the parable of the  workers in the vineyard, at the conclusion of which he repeats the sentiment expressed following his encounter with the young rich man: "So the last will be first, and the first will be last" (20:16). To be precise, Jesus uses the same words but in a different order. On the first occasion, the word order was "first will be last, last will be first." After the parable, the order is, "last will be first, first will be last." In Matthew 19, the focus is the rich – those whom people considered "first." In Matthew 20, the focus is the least – those whom people consider "last."

The workers in the vineyard opens the door to a life that involves "God, me, and others." The outcry of the full-day workers in the parable would be entirely acceptable if not for the opening words of the parable: "For the kingdom of heaven is like . . ." (Matt 20:1). This story reveals the kingdom. In hearing the story, it is easy to get caught up in the claims of unfairness and try to resolve these according to our human sense of justice. But this story is about what "the kingdom of heaven is like." To that end, Jesus told a story that, although it is set in everyday life in the first century, is not an everyday event but a kingdom event.

---

3. Wiesel, *The Trial of God*, vii.
4. Wiesel, vii.

The story gifts us a vision of God and a new view of others. The message of the parable, which is the message of the kingdom, is that it is not for us to offer calculations to show what is fair or unfair. However, it is for us to gaze on the grace, sovereignty, and goodness of God. Because, whether first or last, we also are within God's generous reach. The complaint against the landowner – "You have made them equal to us" (20:12) – is, unexpectedly, what the kingdom of heaven is like. The anger of these workers helps us to see the nature of the kingdom. Their anger shows us that everything is centred on the landowner's – that is, God's – character rather than on the workers' expectations and service. These workers help us see a community of "God, me, and others."

I like how the *South Asia Bible Commentary* sums up this parable:

> And that is the point of the tale: the contrast between those who earned their wage and those who received their wage as an undeserved gift . . . Those who were hired first were paid a just wage, one to which they had agreed, but because God is not only just but also merciful, those who were hired last were paid the same wage. The story sets in balance God's justice and his mercy.[5]

Indeed!

"'The time has come,' [Jesus] said. 'The kingdom of God has come near. Repent and believe the good news!'" (Mark 1:15).

Observation and Discussion

Chapter 2 introduced us to the skills of parable interpretation. Observe how many of those skills have been included in Geoff's preparation of this sermon.

1. "What do we need to know about the first century?" With the Picture, we are drawn into the life of the day labourers. The story slows us down, helping us to see this life more accurately. How is the sense of "I'm interested" developed by doing so?

2. "What is the shock in this parable?" With the Mirror, notice how Geoff lingers with the dialogue in the story. The characters' words are used to speak *for* us and *to* preach to us. How does this draw out the shock and draw attention to "Me!"?

3. "Who is the first person Jesus mentions in this parable?" It is the landowner. This takes us to the Window because the landowner

---

5. Wintle, "Matthew," 1264.

represents God. What is it about the landowner's behaviour that helps us to see God and see his character?

4. "Am I deaf to this parable?" With the Door, notice how the story speaks a message about God and others that is different from the one people tend to gain from a quick first reading. How does our view of "God, me, and others" change?

5. Are there any other skills from chapter 2 that are evident in Geoff's sermon?

10

The Tenants (Matthew 21:33–46)

Wilfredo Weigandt

Creating the Sermon Using the Picture-Mirror-Window-Door Model

After carefully studying Matthew 21:33–46, while bearing in mind the skills for interpreting parables that were discussed in chapter 2, the sermon structure can be created. In the chart (Figure 17), the descriptions which best show the parable moving through the stages of Picture-Mirror-Window-Door are selected. The choices made for this sermon are shown below:

When preaching a parable, look . . .			
at the Picture	*in* the Mirror	*through* the Window	*beyond* the Door
We see life	We see ourselves	We see God	We see others
Sight	Insight	Vision	Imagination
Information	Intimidation	Invitation	Incarnation
Somebody else	Me!	God and me	God, me, and others
I'm interested	I'm shattered	I'm challenged	I'm called
Knowledge	Conviction	Revelation	Response

(Figure 17)

The Sermon
Matthew 21:33–46

³³ "Listen to another parable: There was a landowner who planted a vineyard. He put a wall around it, dug a winepress in it and built a watchtower. Then he rented the vineyard to some farmers and moved to another place. ³⁴ When the harvest time approached, he sent his servants to the tenants to collect his fruit.

³⁵ "The tenants seized his servants; they beat one, killed another, and stoned a third. ³⁶ Then he sent other servants to them, more than the first time, and the tenants treated them the same way. ³⁷ Last of all, he sent his son to them. 'They will respect my son,' he said.

³⁸ "But when the tenants saw the son, they said to each other, 'This is the heir. Come, let's kill him and take his inheritance.' ³⁹ So they took him and threw him out of the vineyard and killed him.

⁴⁰ "Therefore, when the owner of the vineyard comes, what will he do to those tenants?"

⁴¹ "He will bring those wretches to a wretched end," they replied, "and he will rent the vineyard to other tenants, who will give him his share of the crop at harvest time."

⁴² Jesus said to them, "Have you never read in the Scriptures:

> "'The stone the builders rejected
> has become the cornerstone;
> the Lord has done this,
> and it is marvellous in our eyes'?

⁴³ "Therefore I tell you that the kingdom of God will be taken away from you and given to a people who will produce its fruit. ⁴⁴ Anyone who falls on this stone will be broken to pieces; anyone on whom it falls will be crushed."

⁴⁵ When the chief priests and the Pharisees heard Jesus' parables, they knew he was talking about them. ⁴⁶ They looked for a way to arrest him, but they were afraid of the crowd because the people held that he was a prophet.

What a range of expectations! We all have expectations which shape our life in big and small ways. Among many others they might be: the announcement of the new treatment for a disease, looking at the future of our children, smelling freshly baked bread, or coming to the end of a bad year. God also has expectations. The parable that inspires us today presents some of the expectations relating to the place God has given Jesus in his kingdom. Shall we review these together?

When Jesus tells this parable, he is in Jerusalem. To be more specific, he is in the temple, teaching. His presence in the city is highly controversial: from the time of his entrance to Jerusalem, Jesus is acclaimed as the Son of David and blessed as the one "who comes in the name of the Lord," and the people in this capital city are moved and welcome Jesus as "the prophet from Nazareth in Galilee" (Matt 21:1–11). But then, this prophet enters the temple and attacks vendors, money-changers, and merchants, claiming that those responsible for the temple have turned this house of God from a house of prayer into a den of thieves (21:12–13). Sick people approach and Jesus heals them, causing the children of the temple to burst into shouts of praise for his wonderful works (21:14–15). The chief priests and teachers of the law are outraged and protest to Jesus because he lets them shout, "Hosanna to the Son of David!" Jesus confronts them, by quoting part of a psalm in support of the children's praise, then retires for the night to Bethany (21:16–17).

The next day, on his way to Jerusalem, Jesus engages in another prophetic act that is related to the parable he would soon relate. This involves a fig-tree – which is symbolic of Israel – that he finds on his way that does not bear the expected fruits (21:18–22). As he teaches in the temple, Jesus is rebuked by the chief priests and elders of the Jewish people. They question his actions: "By what authority are you doing these things?" (21:23). Jesus surprises them with a challenge-response that defeats his opponents (21:24–27). Against this background, and speaking to this same audience, Jesus continues the dialogue through two parables: the two sons (21:28–32) and the tenants (21:33–44). As a result, the tense climate that existed prior to the telling of these parables intensifies. Our focus is the second of the two parables: the tenants.

Picture: Somebody Else

The parable begins by presenting a picture (21:33–39). The parable is credible, bloody, and accessible to Jesus's opponents – the chief priests and Pharisees. The parable places us in the Palestine conquered by the Roman Empire, where landowners often did not reside on the land but, rather, in Jerusalem or even in Rome. The discontent of the workers who rented and cultivated the land went hand-in-hand with nationalistic pride. A

refusal to pay rent to the absent landlord was often the first step to murdering him and seizing his property.

The story is strong and brutal. It is a work of art created by Jesus and tailored to his audience. But the picture so far does not seem to disturb the chief priests, the teachers of the law, and the elders of the Jewish people. Perhaps they feel that this story does not touch them in any way because it deals with matters far removed from their lives.

- This parable is about an owner who invests in a vineyard and enters into a rental agreement with a group of farmers.
- At harvest time, the owner sends his servants to collect the agreed rent. One of the servants is beaten, another is killed, and another stoned.
- Then the owner sends more servants, who are also mistreated.
- Finally, the owner sends his own son, expecting that he will be respected. However, the tenants murder the son.

The parable speaks of real contexts and situations that Jesus's opponents perceive as being far from their lives. They are temple officials in Jerusalem, not farm labourers. They are leaders of renowned Jewish institutions, not vineyard owners. They are dedicated to the religion of Israel, not to rental agreements. Rereading the parable today, we perceive the disloyal, disrespectful, cruel, violent, unscrupulous, and evil attitude of the farmers. But we also observe the faithful, patient, merciful way the landowner behaves towards the farmers.

Mirror: Intimidation

Then the parable becomes a mirror (21:40–41). Jesus asks a question of the chief priests and Pharisees: "Therefore, when the owner of the vineyard comes, what will he do to those tenants?" (21:40). This exposes the religious leaders.

With his question, Jesus tests their sense of justice and their attitude when an agreement is broken. In other words, Jesus is asking them: What do you think? As leaders of Israel, what do you think the owner should do with the first tenants? What do they deserve? How would you judge the attitude of the tenants? Jesus's audience understand the parable. Their response shows that they catch the flow of the story and participate in the parable: "'He will bring those wretches to a wretched end,' they replied, 'and he will rent the vineyard to other tenants, who will give him his share of the crop at harvest time'" (21:41). There they are; the religious leaders. Obviously, these religious leaders can correctly apply justice. They can clearly discern the breach of an agreement and the consequences that flow from this.

But, my friends, the parable is not only narrative art; it is also a stinging provocation and a surprising challenge. It is the art of unmasking the obvious and confronting the listeners' distance from the parable. Whether they know it or not, whether they sense it or not, Jesus's question is a mirror for his opponents! The parable throws them against themselves! It compels self-criticism! Led by the story of Jesus, the response of the Jewish leaders is a judgement on themselves: the owner of the vineyard should prosecute the tenants, remove them from his field, and hire other tenants who will honour the agreement. As Jesus utters the last words of his reply, the chief priests and Pharisees began to squirm:

- The owner of the vineyard, is it God?
- What!? Do the tenants of the vineyard represent us as the Jewish people and as evil leaders who do not honour the covenant?
- Do the owner's servants perhaps represent the prophets?
- Does the owner's son represent this Jesus who stands in front of us, pretending to be the Messiah?
- Do the tenants who will be given the vineyard represent a new people who will fulfil the covenant?

What is Jesus suggesting by this parable? The mirror has done its work by revealing their identity and compelling them to identify with the parable.

The parable produces "Intimidation."

Now the chief priests, and Pharisees of the Jewish people are perceived within history. And their place in it infuriates them. But they are already named in the parable, and they feel vulnerable.

Window: We See God

In verse 42, Jesus quotes from Psalm 118 to give a window through which to see God. But before analyzing this quotation, consider how God's character has already been beautifully portrayed in the parable:

- As "owner of the vineyard," he is a God who is present and active, who trusts Israel, and who reveals to her what is God's.

- As a "landowner," he is a God who lays the foundations for a healthy relationship with his people and expects them to respond with loyalty and by acting responsibly.
- He is a God who, as a covenant God faithfully carries out his agreement and, despite the mistreatment he receives, seeks a reunion with Israel and who does all he can to achieve reconciliation with his people.

The parable reviews centuries of history that demonstrate both the generosity of God and the rebellion of Israel. The parable presents, with crystal clarity, the reality of that troubled relationship between God and Israel, and even anticipates the future – the death of Jesus at the hands of the Jewish religious leaders of the time. Perhaps, at some point in this parable, the chief priests and Pharisees recognize the similarities between Jesus's parable and Isaiah's "Song of the Vineyard" (Isa 5:1–7), where, although Yahweh had carefully cultivated his vineyard, it yielded only sour grapes. The prophet Isaiah makes the point that the Lord cared for Judah and expected his people to respect the law and act justly. They, however, were guilty of bloodshed.

Could it be that Jesus with his parable updates the poem of Isaiah? Jesus brings Psalm 118:22–23 to the dialogue, and with this he invites them to visualize God:

> [42] Jesus said to them, "Have you never read in the Scriptures:
>
>> "'The stone the builders rejected
>> has become the cornerstone;
>> the Lord has done this,
>> and it is marvellous in our eyes'?" (Matt 21:42)

As in the parable, the language of the psalm is also figurative. The setting is the construction of a temple. The stone discarded and rejected by the builders becomes the foundation stone and, at the same time, orders the entire construction. This is what God does. It is his doing. It has his stamp on it. The stone has its place and, citing the psalm, Jesus points to the Lord as the author of his place in the kingdom of God. What the window shows undoubtedly fills the chief priest and Pharisees with astonishment and indignation. Overwhelmed and shocked, they wonder:

- Do the builders who reject the cornerstone represent us?
- Does the cornerstone represent this Jesus who is arguing with us, and does this mean that he is the Christ?

- Does the one ultimately responsible for building the temple – who accepts and affirms the cornerstone and rejects those who discard it – represent God?
- Could it be that God himself legitimizes what we reject?

Door: I'm Called

In verses 43 and 44, we have a door. A call is presented. Jesus makes it clear that the path that Israel had taken up to this point did not please God. The true people of the Lord must cultivate other attitudes and actions.

> "Therefore I tell you that the kingdom of God will be taken away from you and given to a people who will produce its fruit. Anyone who falls on this stone will be broken to pieces; anyone on whom it falls will be crushed." (Matt 21:43–44)

The people of God are those who bear fruit in keeping with the kingdom of God. Simple. Direct. Overwhelming. Therefore, Israel's conduct does not meet God's expectations. But the call to Israel – and to any other people – continues because God is still looking for a people. He rejects those who do not bear fruit for his kingdom, yes; but he also invites others to form a people who will honour his character. A distinctive feature of this people is that they do not stumble by fighting, disputing with, or resisting Jesus; on the contrary, they recognize Jesus and love him. The end of this story answers the earlier question of the chief priests and the elders of the people: "Jesus entered the temple courts, and, while he was teaching, the chief priests and the elders of the people came to him. 'By what authority are you doing these things?' they asked. 'And who gave you this authority?'" (21:23). Through the parable, Jesus declares that God himself has given him that authority by setting him as the foundation stone.

Thus, through a harsh but fruitful dialogue, the parable reminded the ruling classes of the temple-state in Jerusalem that God created through his covenant with Israel. That covenant was fertilized with confidence, patience, new opportunities, mercy, faithfulness; and, by virtue of his grace, God waited for the fruits of the kingdom from his beloved people. Israel, with their legalism, did not live up to the Lord's expectations and did not even recognize Jesus as the central character in the kingdom of God. For this reason, the Lord took that place away from Israel and opened it to another people who do honour him with the fruits of the kingdom. Why would Matthew have included this parable in his gospel? Why was it relevant to him? Did he want to make his contribution to the question of the opening of the kingdom of God to the Gentiles through the work of Christ among the Jewish communities to whom he was writing? How might this parable have been read in their synagogues in the Roman Empire in the first century?

Could this parable have been used in another intimidating, provocative, and subversive context that marked a decisive step in the establishment of a new people of God? Could this parable have been the basis of a message for a young church in the early years after Jesus's ascension? This text could well have been instrumental in breaking down the wall that separated Jews and Gentiles and assigning Jesus the central place in the kingdom of God. I think it very likely that the apostle Paul had this parable in mind when he wrote to the believers in Ephesus:

> [11] Therefore, remember that formerly you who are Gentiles by birth and called "uncircumcised" by those who call themselves "the circumcision" (which is done in the body by human hands) – [12] remember that at that time you were separate from Christ, excluded from citizenship in Israel and foreigners to the covenants of the promise, without hope and without God in the world. [13] But now in Christ Jesus you who once were far away have been brought near by the blood of Christ.
>
> [14] For he himself is our peace, who has made the two groups one and has destroyed the barrier, the dividing wall of hostility, [15] by setting aside in his flesh the law with its commands and regulations. His purpose was to create in himself one new humanity out of the two, thus making peace, [16] and in one body to reconcile both of them to God through the cross, by which he put to death their hostility. [17] He came and preached peace to you who were far away and peace to those who were near. [18] For through him we both have access to the Father by one Spirit.
>
> [19] Consequently, you are no longer foreigners and strangers, but fellow citizens with God's people and also members of his household, [20] built on the foundation of the apostles and prophets, with Christ Jesus himself as the chief cornerstone. [21] In him the whole building is joined together and rises to become a holy temple in the Lord. [22] And in him you too are being built together to become a dwelling in which God lives by his Spirit. (Eph 2:11–22)

Could it be that Paul with his speech, applies Jesus's parable which had in turn applied the poem of Isaiah? God opened the door. God made it possibile for all people – Jews and Gentiles alike – to be reconciled to him and to each other. God forms all those who bear the fruits of his kingdom into one body, one people, one kingdom. God made the prophets and the apostles the foundation of this new humanity – the family of God and his holy temple. Through their connection with Christ – who is the cornerstone – and the help of the Holy Spirit, believers bear the fruits of God's kingdom. Now, what does this text tell us here and now?

This parable challenges us, as leaders and as a community of faith, to consider our response to God's expectations and the place we give to Jesus as the example of life in his kingdom. Do we know what God expects of us? Do we know what God expects of us as leaders? Do we know what God expects of us as we serve his mission for his church? If we don't know, it is important to pray for clarity so that we can understand our place in God's plan and act accordingly. If we know, are we aligning our lives with God's expectations? Are fruits of the kingdom evident in our lives?

This parable, and the chief priests and Pharisees, become a warning to put the church on guard against remaining unproductive and sterile. Let's take up the challenge of the parable. Let's review our response to God's expectations and the place we give Jesus as the example of life in his kingdom.

Let us produce a harvest of righteousness in God's vineyard!

Observation and Discussion

Let's continue with the same approach but look for evidence of Wilfredo working with skills of interpretation that were not mentioned in chapter 9.

1. "What was happening when Jesus told this parable?" After the Scripture reading, notice how Wilfredo takes time to explain "the tense climate that existed prior to the telling of these parables" before taking us into life in Palestine in the first century with the Picture. How do these sections work together to have us think the parable is about "Somebody Else"?

2. "What difference does Jesus make?" Jesus *is* the difference. It is his question that holds up the Mirror for his listeners. Wilfredo then adds even more questions to recreate the "stinging provocation" and help us feel the "Intimidation."

3. "How does the OT heritage feed the NT parables?" With the Window, Wilfredo lingers with this heritage, helping us see the allegories that are at work here. This prepares the way for the shock in the parable. When it comes to "We see God," what is the surprising place in which God is found?

4. "What are the major themes?" With the Door, watch for the suggestion that the poetry of Isaiah 5 is applied in the parable of Jesus, which, in turn, is applied in Paul's writings (Eph 2:11–22). How does this bring the parable into the reality of "I'm called" and our own Christian discipleship experience?

5. "What type of parable is this?" This is the only question from chapter 2 that we have not mentioned so far in our discussion of the parables of Jesus. How would you respond?

11

The Friend at Midnight (Luke 11:5–13)

Geoff New

Creating the Sermon Using the Picture-Mirror-Window-Door Model

After carefully studying Luke 11:5–13, bearing in mind the skills for interpreting parables that were discussed in chapter 2, the sermon structure can be created. In the chart (Figure 18), the descriptions that best show the parable moving through the stages of Picture-Mirror-Window-Door are selected. The choices made for this sermon are shown below:

When preaching a parable, look . . .			
at the Picture	*in* the Mirror	*through* the Window	*beyond* the Door
We see life	We see ourselves	We see God	We see others
Sight	Insight	Vision	Imagination
Information	Intimidation	Invitation	Incarnation
Somebody else	Me!	God and me	God, me, and others
I'm interested	I'm shattered	I'm challenged	I'm called
Knowledge	Conviction	Revelation	Response

(Figure 18)

The Sermon
Luke 11:5–13

⁵ Then Jesus said to them, "Suppose you have a friend, and you go to him at midnight and say, 'Friend, lend me three loaves of bread; ⁶ a friend of mine on a journey has come to me, and I have no food to offer him.' ⁷ And suppose the one inside answers, 'Don't bother me. The door is already locked, and my children and I are in bed. I can't get up and give you anything.' ⁸ I tell you, even though he will not get up and give you the bread because of friendship, yet because of your shameless audacity he will surely get up and give you as much as you need.

⁹ "So I say to you: Ask and it will be given to you; seek and you will find; knock and the door will be opened to you. ¹⁰ For everyone who asks receives; the one who seeks finds; and to the one who knocks, the door will be opened.

¹¹ "Which of you fathers, if your son asks for a fish, will give him a snake instead? ¹² Or if he asks for an egg, will give him a scorpion? ¹³ If you then, though you are evil, know how to give good gifts to your children, how much more will your Father in heaven give the Holy Spirit to those who ask him!"

Picture: Information

I will always remember the moment. My wife, one of my sons, and I were relaxing at home one night. Suddenly, there was loud knocking at the front door. I quickly went to answer the door; when I opened it, there were two police officers. The urgency of their knocking, that it was night, and the fact that the police do not normally arrive at your door with good news all combined to leave me bewildered and fearful. They were there because of a family emergency, but all finally turned out well. At least it was only 8:00 p.m., and my family and I were awake when the hammering at our door started. In the parable before us, it was midnight, and the family were asleep. How much more would the initial fright have been to be woken from a deep sleep at midnight by urgent knocking at their door (11:5)?

Night. Urgency. Need.

Yet, the way Jesus tells the parable is playful and humorous. He has just responded to the disciples' request to teach them how to pray by teaching them the Lord's Prayer (Luke 11:2–4). After teaching them *what* to pray, he now teaches them *how* they ought to approach their Father in heaven. The way Jesus tells the story might be expressed like this: "This would never happen – but imagine if it did?!" The background Jesus paints gives us information about a serious situation, but the way events play out is so unlikely that it is laughable.

Imagine a traveller arriving late at night and the host not having enough food to feed him (11:6). In biblical times, such a situation would not just have been slightly embarrassing but deeply shameful. Hosting a visitor was not just the cultural thing to do, it was the sacred thing to do – even if that person was a stranger. There was no choice. Regardless of the lateness of the hour, food had to be found. Bread was baked daily for that day's meals; once it was gone, there were no late-night shops to go to, only sleeping neighbours. The friend needs the usual portion of food for a meal – three loaves of bread (11:5). He is so desperate that he doesn't ask the neighbour to give him the bread but to "lend" it to him (11:5). He will do whatever it takes: "Give me the bread now and I'll get it back to you somehow!" If ever a parable was comedy, this is it.

The parable does not actually say that the friend knocked on the door; it only records the conversation between the friend at the door and the reluctant friend inside (11:5–7). Nevertheless, Jesus's ask-seek-knock application of the parable (11:9–10) and the description of the friend as having "shameless audacity" (11:8) give us important information. I imagine the friend did not hold back. Since he needed help and needed it now, I imagine he knocked on the door. Given the internal layout of the house and the external proximity of houses in first-century villages in Palestine, his pleas and knocking raise the tension in the story.

Consider the internal layout of the one-roomed houses of Jesus's time. Families would often lie on the same sleeping mat, and even the animals might be sheltered inside the house. The sleepy neighbour getting up, stepping over sleeping children, and unbolting the door was a sure way to wake up the household (11:7). And if that didn't wake them, fumbling around in the dark trying to light a lamp and find the bread certainly would! Not only were the children of the house at risk of being woken, so was the village. The external proximity of houses in the village meant that the neighbours would not stay asleep long either. *The Message* translation captures this thought well: "If you stand your ground, knocking and waking all the neighbors, he'll finally get up and get you whatever you need" (11:8). As one Bible commentator helpfully points out, "The conventions of hospitality involve not only the person surprised by his traveling friend but also the whole village in the need to provide a respectable meal. The need of the would-be host thus becomes the need of the village."[1] Everyone's reputation is at risk. If this traveller is not fed, word would spread about the failure of this community and its members to welcome a visitor. If online reviews existed in the first century, they would be facing a one-star-out-of-five review, accompanied by a brutal description of what had happened. And so, Jesus presents a realistic first-century setting with the utterly unlikely problem of a sleepy neighbour reluctant to respond to the need to provide hospitality.

Then, into this story, Jesus casts a person – you.

Mirror: We See Ourselves

Jesus tells this parable in the form of a long question. He asks, "Suppose you have a friend, and you go to him at midnight . . . and suppose the one inside answers . . . 'I can't get up and give you anything'" (11:5, 7). The parable is asking, "What would *you* do in this situation?" Jesus put everyone who hears this parable in the leading role. We are at once in the centre of the action. We are cast as the friend in desperate need in the dead of night, waking up our neighbour and pleading for help.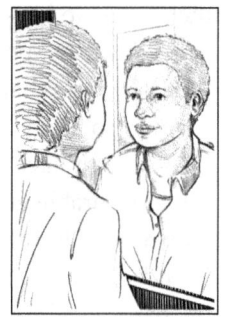

In this parable, it is inescapable – "We see ourselves."

For some reason, I had always misread this parable. Perhaps I rushed the reading of it. But I always misheard it as Jesus placing me inside the house, asleep with my children, and then the neighbour arriving and waking me up, wanting bread. That was convenient because it put distance between me and the point Jesus is making in this story. This kind of mishearing of the parable that I was guilty of excuses me from seeing myself in the mirror of this parable. Jesus will not have that. You and I have an active role in this parable.

You receive the first shock: a late-night guest arrives. It's an unexpected visit from a friend on a journey! You receive the second shock: you have no food to put before him. Jesus places you and me standing at the door at midnight in need. "And suppose the one inside answers, 'Don't bother me. The door is already locked, and my children and I are in bed. I can't get up and give you anything'" (11:7). This is the third shock. Our neighbour would never give such

---

1. Green, *Luke*, 448.

an answer. Not in first-century Palestine. But Jesus is asking us to imagine, "What if it did? What would you do?"

Your answer reveals your heart of prayer.

Regarding the friend in the parable, Jesus provides the answer so that we can compare our response: "I tell you, even though he will not get up and give you the bread because of friendship, yet because of your shameless audacity he will surely get up and give you as much as you need" (11:8). "Shameless audacity." Or, to put it in other words, the friend at midnight showed boldness without feeling shame. In such a situation, how would Jesus describe you? If your neighbour refused to get out of bed and give you bread, would you return home or stand your ground? Given that Jesus has you as the central character in his parable, he is revealing your heart. Jesus's parable is mining your soul to see how you pray. So, if Jesus was to tell this parable using your name, what prayer quality would he attribute to you? The parable provides a means by which "We see ourselves."

> Suppose [your name] had a friend, and [your name] went to him at midnight . . . I tell you . . . because of your [specific prayer quality] he will surely get up and give you as much as you need.

How would Jesus describe the nature of your prayer? Would Jesus say you had "shameless audacity"? Or would he say something else?

"Timid uncertainty"?

"Faltering faith"?

"Deep trust"?

"Confident approach"?

"Abundant hope"?

"Determined wrestling"?

Your answer is found in the quality of your current prayer life.

As you look in the mirror of this parable, you might be discouraged by what you see or you may be heartened and affirmed. Either way, the message is that Jesus wants you to continue to grow in "shameless audacity" in prayer. Through this parable, with you as the central character, he is saying, "Ask and it will be given to you . . . For everyone who asks receives" (11:9–10).

Window: God and Me

We have seen how this parable says, "You are like the friend at midnight." In doing so, it questions us about how we approach God. It examines our faith. We compare ourselves to the friend at midnight.

The first person Jesus mentions in a parable is often the person to whom he wants you to relate. But not on this occasion. The first person mentioned in this parable is nothing like God. The parable does not give the message that God is like the sleeping neighbour. God does not need to be woken up to answer our prayers. Such a view of God is the kind of belief that Elijah mocked in his confrontation with the prophets of Baal and Asherah on Mount Carmel (1 Kgs 18:16-40). Those prophets called on Baal to rain down fire on their sacrifice, but nothing happened. So Elijah taunted them: "'Shout louder!' he said. 'Surely he is a god! Perhaps he is deep in thought, or busy, or travelling. Maybe he is sleeping and must be awakened'" (18:27). To approach our Father in heaven thinking that we need to stir him into action and convince him to answer us is to act more like a prophet of Baal than a disciple of Jesus Christ.

This parable gifts us a vision of "God and me."

God is not like that sleepy, reluctant neighbour. Immediately after this parable, Jesus uses another image to drive home the message of the friend at midnight. He is concerned that we are clear about the nature of our Father in heaven. He is concerned that we are clear about what to expect from him. So, Jesus says that no human father would give his son a snake or a scorpion when they ask for a fish or an egg (Luke 11:11-12). If we, as flawed humans, know how to give good gifts to our children, how much more will our Father in heaven do so (11:13)? This second case study emphasizes the nature of God and the way he responds to us.

This parable is a how-much-more parable that contrasts God with the reluctant neighbour. It presents a lesser personality who finally does the right thing to highlight the greater personality who always does the right thing. If a sleepy, reluctant neighbour finally responds to a friend at his door at midnight, how much more will your Father in heaven respond to you? As mentioned earlier, this parable is in the form of a question – a question that asks what you would do if you did not receive what you need (11:5-7). Having asked the question, the parable answers it by presenting the neighbour as being motivated into action by your boldness (11:8). The question and answer that the parable presents is a vision of the nature of your relationship with God. This parable is a call to you to grow in your spiritual practice of prayer and your knowledge of who it is that you are praying to. This parable is an exciting vision of what awaits you when your need is great and the night is dark.

> "Seek and you will find . . . for . . . the one who seeks finds." (11:9–10)

This parable is a word from Jesus about who he wants you to become. He wants you to be someone who has "shameless audacity" when praying. He wants you to approach boldly your heavenly Father who gives good gifts (11:13). As the central character in the parable, he wants you to be able to say, "This story is a vision of 'God and me.'"

Door: Response

The parable uses an everyday item – bread – as the essential need. The provision of bread was as much about ensuring that the friend at midnight kept his honour as it was about feeding a late-night visitor. The provision of bread was as much about ensuring that the humanity of the host was kept intact as it was about satisfying the visitor's hunger.

In addition, the parable is set at night. In the gospels, wherever night is linked to prayer, we see an interesting pattern. Jesus prayed at night (Luke 6:12), and the disciples failed to pray at night (Luke 22:39–46). The parable creates a situation which has you in great need, unable to serve others, with your dignity as a person under threat. The parable also presents a solution: "Knock and the door will be opened . . . for . . . to the one who knocks, the door will be opened" (11:9–10). What is your response?

When applying and explaining the parable, Jesus concludes with "how much more will your Father in heaven give the Holy Spirit to those who ask him!" (11:13), making it clear that our most essential need is the Holy Spirit, who empowers us to serve others and to pray with "shameless audacity" because we know that our Father in heaven gives good gifts to those who ask. What is your response to this? Given that the parable is set in the middle of the night, maybe the message is that you need to wake up. Maybe you need to be roused from your sleep because there are visitors at your door, needing to be hosted and fed. Maybe you need to wake up to the lack in your life that can only be filled by the good gift of the Holy Spirit.

Be bold in your asking because Jesus makes the parable true.

I love how one Bible commentator describes this by saying that both the parable and Jesus's final explanation of it "state the obvious – but only on the assumption that God is 'friend' and 'father' to humankind. For this very reason, they can only come from the mouth of Jesus."[2]

> So friend, "Knock and the door will be opened . . . for . . . to the one who knocks, the door will be opened."

Observation and Discussion

With this sermon, let's practice working with the chart (Figure 18 above) by engaging with the words and phrases chosen to describe the journey through the parable.

1. Notice the tension in the "Information" section. Geoff describes experiences that could happen in any culture at any time, while also pointing out distinctive features of the foreign context of Palestine in the first century. What are some examples of these features?

2. "Jesus puts everyone who hears this parable in the leading role." Listen carefully to the discussion about whether this role is inside or outside the house. What difference does this make as "We see ourselves" in the parable?

3. A common challenge for today's preacher is to sharpen the shock again. How does Geoff use self-disclosure about his own mistakes, as well as focus on questions Jesus might ask, to recover that shock?

4. Rather than God being likened to the first person in the story in an allegorical way, he is contrasted with that person in a "how-much-more" manner. What does this mean? How does this impact the "God and me" relationship?

5. Notice how the sermon sets this parable in the context of what Luke places immediately before and after the parable. As is often the case in the gospels, how does this literary context help shape our "Response" to the parable?

---

2. Schweizer, *Luke*, 193.

12

The Rich Fool (Luke 12:13–21)

Geoff New

Creating the Sermon Using the Picture-Mirror-Window-Door Model

After carefully studying Luke 12:13–21, bearing in mind the skills for interpreting the parables that were discussed in chapter 2, the sermon structure can be created. In the chart (Figure 19), the descriptions that best show the parable moving through the stages of Picture-Mirror-Window-Door are selected. The choices made for this sermon are shown below:

When preaching a parable, look . . .			
at the Picture	*in* the Mirror	*through* the Window	*beyond* the Door
We see life	We see ourselves	We see God	We see others
Sight	Insight	Vision	Imagination
Information	Intimidation	Invitation	Incarnation
Somebody else	Me!	God and me	God, me, and others
I'm interested	I'm shattered	I'm challenged	I'm called
Knowledge	Conviction	Revelation	Response

(Figure 19)

The Sermon
Luke 12:13–21

¹³ Someone in the crowd said to him, "Teacher, tell my brother to divide the inheritance with me."

¹⁴ Jesus replied, "Man, who appointed me a judge or an arbiter between you?" ¹⁵ Then he said to them, "Watch out! Be on your guard against all kinds of greed; life does not consist in an abundance of possessions."

¹⁶ And he told them this parable: "The ground of a certain rich man yielded an abundant harvest. ¹⁷ He thought to himself, 'What shall I do? I have no place to store my crops.'

¹⁸ "Then he said, 'This is what I'll do. I will tear down my barns and build bigger ones, and there I will store my surplus grain. ¹⁹ And I'll say to myself, "You have plenty of grain laid up for many years. Take life easy; eat, drink and be merry."'

²⁰ "But God said to him, 'You fool! This very night your life will be demanded from you. Then who will get what you have prepared for yourself?'

²¹ "This is how it will be with whoever stores up things for themselves but is not rich towards God."

Picture: Somebody Else

"Meanwhile, when a crowd of many thousands had gathered, so that they were trampling on one another, Jesus began to speak first to his disciples . . ." (Luke 12:1). And so, Jesus begins an extended time of teaching (12:1–13:9), sometimes addressing his disciples, other times the crowd; sometimes addressing a smaller group, sometimes an individual. Yet, regardless of who Jesus is talking to, the crowd listens. We, too, listen.

Jesus begins by talking to his disciples (12:1–12). He warns against the hypocrisy of the Pharisees. Then he tells his disciples not to fear those who have the power to martyr them but, rather, to fear God who has the authority to judge after death. He talks about the value God places on them and urges them not to be afraid. Next, he challenges them to bear witness to the Son of Man, warns them against sinning against the Holy Spirit, and assures them that the Spirit will empower them in times of persecution. His teaching deals with integrity, fear, God's protection, and courage in declaring the name of Christ. All this is what it means to follow Jesus.

Suddenly, someone in the crowd interrupts him: "Teacher, tell my brother to divide the inheritance with me" (12:13). Hasn't this man listened to anything Jesus has said?! The man's intrusion is jarring. He has totally changed the subject. The earlier description of thousands trampling on one another as they gathered around Jesus (12:1) provides a fitting picture of the man's interruption. With his words, the man engages in a different kind of trampling. Two brothers are trampling each other over their inheritance. And the man tramples on Jesus's teaching with his self-absorbed demand that Jesus rule in his favour.

The man's hope that Jesus would judge between his brother and himself was not an uncommon expectation. People would often ask a rabbi to rule on such matters. Indeed, rabbis would say that if one heir wanted part of the inheritance, it should be given. The man is demanding that Jesus declare what any other rabbi would have done. But this man has not approached just any rabbi. Jesus's answer is blunt: "Man, who appointed me a judge or an arbiter between you?" (12:14). Jesus refuses to be drawn into this family fight. He addresses everyone there: "Watch out! Be on your guard against all kinds of greed; life does not consist in an abundance of possessions" (12:15). Jesus uses the interruption to highlight what he had just been talking about to his disciples. People can live small and greedy lives without giving any thought to eternal things or to God himself.

As a pastor, I have been aware of families caught up in bitter arguments over inheritances. I know of incidents where family members have stood on either side of the coffin during a funeral, yelling at each other, "You are not getting any of the inheritance!" A funeral director once told me about being summoned to the home of someone he had never met. He thought he was being called because someone had died. When he arrived, however, the man who had called him led him into a large room. There, seated around the room, was a gathering of the man's family. The man announced, "This is the funeral director who will oversee my funeral when I die. He is here today to witness me signing my will. None of you are getting a thing in my will!"

Jesus tells the crowd a parable about a "certain rich man" (12:16). This is a story about "Somebody else." Most if not all those in the crowd would never have experienced the kind of life the rich man in the parable enjoyed. They could listen to this parable without fear of being challenged – or so they thought. The rich man has a bumper crop. His wealth has increased by genuine means – he has not cheated or taken advantage of anyone. He decides to tear down his barns and replace them with bigger barns to store the grain (12:16–18). He has secured a future of leisure (12:19). But did he need to build bigger barns? If he had sold all his crop after the harvest, the surplus would have been in the local market and not in his barns. The price of grain would have dropped, helping the buyers – although not him, as the seller. Perhaps that is why he chose to store his surplus grain – to hold it back until there was a future shortage and he could gain a better price. It is not without reason that Proverbs states, "People curse the one who hoards grain, but they pray God's blessing on the one who is willing to sell" (Prov 11:26). In contrast, in the OT, Joseph stored grain in preparation for a crippling famine rather than for his personal comfort (Gen 41:47–49, 53–57).

The rich man has a problem – a bumper crop. However, the solution he proposes reveals his real problem – his belief that life consists in an abundance of possessions (12:15). Such a belief is godless, as the rich man was about to discover, quite unexpectedly, just like all who hear this parable and think that its message does not apply to them because they assume it is about "Somebody else."

Mirror: Conviction

When confronted with an abundant harvest, the rich man asks a question on which the whole parable turns: "What shall I do?" (12:17). Our true heart is probably revealed more in times of plenty than in times of poverty. Francis of Assisi, who lived over eight hundred years ago, was from a very rich Italian family. As a young man, he lived a wild life. One night, while partying with friends, he went missing for about thirty minutes. To this day, no one knows exactly what happened; but when his friends found him, he was a different person. Francis told them  that he had encountered the most beautiful woman he had ever met – "Lady Poverty." Francis had not met a physical person but was describing a deeply spiritual encounter that resulted in his dramatic change of heart. From that moment, Francis dedicated himself to Christ and renounced his vast fortune. He served lepers, cared for the poor, and preached the gospel. He is known in church history as *Il Poverello* – "little poor man" – and people began to call him "God's little poor man." From a position of plenty, Francis answered the question "What shall I do?" and began to follow Christ. The rich man in the parable, however, answered differently and responded differently.

The rich man talks to himself, and his conversation reveals how self-centred he is. He uses the words "I" and "my" at least ten times – for example, "my crops," "my barns," "my surplus grain," "I will tear down," "I will store," and "I'll say to myself." It is one thing to think through a problem; it is quite another to create a solution as if you have the power of life and death.

"What shall I do?"

The rich man could have expanded his world and enriched others; instead, in his greed, he shrank his world: "Take life easy; eat, drink and be merry" (12:19). But he was mistaken. His abundance of possessions revealed the poverty of his heart and his failure to acknowledge God: "But God said to him, 'You fool! This very night your life will be demanded from you. Then who will get what you have prepared for yourself?'" (12:20). In the Bible, the word "fool" has a range of meanings. While "fool" can refer to someone who is immoral, it sometimes refers to a person who does not have wisdom. Here, in Jesus's parable, its meaning is what usually comes to mind when we hear the word "fool" – the man was just plain stupid!

Jesus told this parable as a response to the man who had interrupted his teaching. In the parable, God interrupted the rich man's thinking, plans, and life dramatically and finally. Similarly, Jesus interrupted the life of the man demanding his inheritance. Jesus's parable had a message for that man – you are being stupid! As one Bible commentator notes, if Jesus had granted the man's request and told the brother to give him the inheritance, the true problem would remain[1] – the man would still be greedy.

How is this parable interrupting your life?

The question "What shall I do?" must be asked with the awareness that God might answer it for you. The question might be answered by you experiencing the conviction of the Holy Spirit. God's words in the parable make plain sense in the life of the man who wanted all the inheritance (12:13). God's words in the parable make plain sense in our lives. "What shall I do?" Would your answer cause God to say, "You are stupid"?

After this parable, Jesus continues his teaching, speaking about our habit of worrying about our lives. He talks about our heavenly Father's care, placing this against the kind of concerns that prompted this parable.

> [32] "Do not be afraid, little flock, for your Father has been pleased to give you the kingdom. [33] Sell your possessions and give to the poor. Provide purses for yourselves that will not wear out, a treasure

---

1. Bailey, *Through Peasant Eyes*, 62.

in heaven that will never fail, where no thief comes near and no moth destroys. ³⁴ For where your treasure is, there your heart will be also." (Luke 12:32–34)

"What shall I do" in the aftermath of blessing? The rich man turned inwards, looking at himself, instead of outwards to others and upwards to God. The rich man had a vision of himself for many years to come (12:19); but he needed a vision of God here and now. We need a vision of God here and now. This parable provides such a vision and convicts our greed.

Window: I'm Challenged

About five hundred years ago, a prominent spiritual leader of the church wrote, "All the things in this world are also created because of God's love and they become a context of gifts, presented to us so that we can know God more easily and make a return of love readily."² The parable begins and ends with the reality of God's gifts.

The rich man was so self-absorbed that he did not see that his abundant harvest was a gift from God. "The ground . . . yielded an abundant harvest" (12:16). Through creation, God had blessed the rich man. At the end of the parable, God said, "This very night your life will be demanded from you" (12:20). The clear message is that the rich man's life had been on loan and that it belonged to God.

This message is all the louder in that this is the only parable where God plays an active role. God speaks directly and plainly from the story. God speaks directly to the rich man in the parable. God speaks directly to the crowd to whom Jesus was telling the parable. God speaks directly to the man who wanted the inheritance. God speaks directly to you. The testimony of the Scriptures is that God gifts us and that we must live remembering this truth. To do otherwise is to be a fool. In this, "I'm challenged."

When he received news of a family tragedy, Job, even in his grief, worshipped God, remembering both the gifts and the sovereignty of God:

> "Naked I came from my mother's womb,
>   and naked I shall depart.

---

2. A current day translation of the words of Ignatius of Loyola (c. 1991/93–1556) in Fleming, *What is Ignatian Spirituality?*, 2.

> The LORD gave and the LORD has taken away;
> may the name of the LORD be praised." (Job 1:21)

King David was once in a position where he could have said the same thing as the rich man in the parable. However, David chose to build God a house rather than build a bigger house for himself (2 Sam 7:1–3). God responded by saying that he would build David a "house" (2 Sam 7:4–16). This house was a dynasty of kings, and this promise was fulfilled in Jesus, the King of kings. David then made plans to build a temple in Jerusalem. After the people of God gave generously towards this temple, King David prayed, "But who am I, and who are my people, that we should be able to give as generously as this? Everything comes from you, and we have given you only what comes from your hand" (1 Chr 29:14). David understood that life and all it holds are gifts from God.

Centuries later, the apostle Paul wrote to the people of God in Corinth: "What do you have that you did not receive? And if you did receive it, why do you boast as though you did not?" (1 Cor 4:7). Paul understood that life and all it holds are gifts from God.

In times of plenty, in what direction does your mind go? How does God feature in your thinking and plans about the future? Are you challenged to see your life as being under the rule and grace of God? Or do you see yourself as being in charge of your life?

Door: Response

Having declared to the rich man that he would die that very night, God's last words to him are, "Then who will get what you have prepared for yourself?" (12:20). Jesus's stern warnings on either side of the parable reinforce this message: "Watch out! Be on your guard against all kinds of greed; life does not consist in an abundance of possessions" (12:14) and, after the parable, "This is how it will be with whoever stores up things for themselves but is not rich towards God" (12:21). The tragedy is that although the man had received an abundance from God,  he did not live abundantly for God. He lived thinking that life consisted "in an abundance of possessions" (12:15). One Bible commentator helpfully sums up Jesus's message to the man who demanded his inheritance, as well as to us who hear this parable: Jesus "came to bring people to God, not to bring property to people."³ God confronts the rich man with the question "Who will get what you have prepared for yourself?" (12:20).

Kenneth Bailey was a missionary in the Middle East for forty years. His work on the parables is particularly noteworthy for his insights into what life would have been like in Jesus's day. Bailey rewords the question in Luke 12:20 for our benefit, to help us understand this more clearly:

> There is no accusing question, such as, "What have you done for others?" or "Why have you failed to help those in need?" or "Why are there no family and friends close to you who would be the natural recipients of your wealth?" . . . Rather, God thunders: look at what you have done to yourself! You plan alone, build alone, indulge alone, and now you will die alone!⁴

What is our "response"?

This parable is placed in what is known as the "Travel Narrative" (Luke 9:51–19:44) in the Gospel of Luke. This section of the gospel tells the story of Jesus travelling towards Jerusalem and the cross. The closer Jesus gets to Jerusalem, the more the opposition against him grows, and the darker the shadow of the cross. So, this parable of the rich fool needs to be heard bearing in mind that Jesus tells this story as he draws nearer to the cross.

Based on this parable, there are two choices: take life easy or take up a cross. What is your "response"?

Based on this parable, there are two economies: being rich towards yourself or being rich towards God.

Which economy are you investing in?

There is one more question that this parable presents: What awaits you "this very night"?

Observation and Discussion

As with the sermon in chapter 11, let's continue to work with the chart (Figure 19 above) by engaging with the words and phrases chosen to describe the journey through the parable.

1. Once again, the foundation of the sermon is built around noticing cultural practices from the historical context as well as insights into the literary context in which Luke has placed the parable. Observing

---

3. Morris, *Luke*, 232.
4. Bailey, *Through Peasant Eyes*, 67.

these details in *every* Bible passage is a crucial skill for the preacher today. Where, in this sermon, does Geoff demonstrate this skill?

2. Notice how the Mirror section is set up by a statement made in the earlier Picture section: "They could listen to this parable without fear of being challenged." Jesus designed this parable to be about "Somebody else." How quickly things change! "What shall I do?" is a confronting question; and Jesus telling a story in which God calls someone a fool – literally, "stupid" – is also confrontational. How does Geoff move us from this character in the parable to the listener today and bring "Conviction" to our lives?

3. This is "the only parable where God plays an active role." Does that surprise you? How does this make the view through the Window – "I'm challenged" – even more immediate and striking?

4. Geoff takes a risk that every preacher must consider. He moves outside the story of the parable to include a story from the life of St. Francis and also moves elsewhere in the Bible to illustrate this parable. The danger in moving outside the parable is that listeners may not return with us to the story. What do you think? Does what Geoff does detract from the parable or illuminate it?

5. Right at the end, in the "Response," notice how an attempt is made to relate the shocking demise of the rich fool to our own lives. The statement directed to him in the parable is now rephrased as a question for today's listeners: "What awaits you this very night?" Do you agree or disagree that this is being faithful to the biblical text? Why?

13

The Lost Coin (Luke 15:8–10)

Esteban Améstegui

Creating the Sermon Using the Picture-Window-Mirror-Door Model

After carefully studying Luke 15:8–10, bearing in mind the skills for interpreting the parables that were discussed in chapter 2, the sermon structure can be created. The chart (Figure 20) depicts the descriptions that best show the parable moving through the four stages. However, for this sermon, note that instead of Picture-Mirror-Window-Door, the author has changed the order to Picture-Window-Mirror-Door, demonstrating how changing the order can sometimes expand and deepen this model of preaching even further.

When preaching a parable, look . . .			
at the Picture	*through* the Window	*in* the Mirror	*beyond* the Door
We see life	We see God	We see ourselves	We see others
Sight	Vision	Insight	Imagination
Information	Invitation	Intimidation	Incarnation
Somebody else	God and me	Me!	God, me, and others
I'm interested	I'm challenged	I'm shattered	I'm called
Knowledge	Revelation	Conviction	Response

(Figure 20)

The Sermon

Have you ever lost an item of great personal value? Perhaps it was something that someone important in your life gave you. Or perhaps it was a memory of a loved one – your partner's engagement ring, the necklace your mother gave you, that old photo of your father you keep in your wallet, or that bracelet you exchanged with your best friend the last time you saw each other.

Recall the panic you felt when you realized that this item was missing. It is very likely that, immediately afterwards, you would have done anything to find this lost item – going to all the places you had been with it, inspecting every inch of the floor, opening all the drawers where it could possibly be, even calling your family and friends to tell them about your problem and ask for their help.

How long did you search? Minutes? Hours? Days? Weeks? Was it hard to think of anything other than finding this thing you had lost? What did you feel when you finally found it? Surely you told all your friends that you had finally found what you had been looking for!

Before we talk about a similar story, let me give a little background that will help you understand the story better.

Picture: Information

Large crowds followed Jesus as he walked along (Luke 14:25). Many of these people were people of ill-repute, like tax collectors and sinners, and so, the religious leaders began to criticize Jesus: "This man welcomes sinners and eats with them" (Luke 15:1–2).

The Pharisees and teachers of the law were well known for their pride. Jesus told a parable about a Pharisee who prayed aloud in the synagogue, "God, I thank you that I am not like other people – robbers, evildoers, adulterers – or even like this tax collector" (Luke 18:11). The Talmud included this prayer, which was prayed frequently at that time: "Blessed are you, Lord, because you have not created me a pagan, nor have you made me a woman or ignorant." Their rejection of others – whether foreigners, women, tax collectors, or sinners – characterized the Jewish religious leaders of the time.

Perhaps the only comparable precedent in the OT was the prophet Jonah, who, when God sent him to Nineveh to preach, ran away to Tarshish. After being rescued from certain death in the sea and kept safe in the belly of a great fish, he went to the city of his enemies, preached and saw the repentance of the authorities and the people, and yet still felt a deep hatred against God's mercy, to the point that he preferred to be dead (Jonah 4:8).

When Jesus heard what the religious leaders were saying about him, he told them three stories. Here is one of them:

Luke 15:8–10

> ⁸ "Or suppose a woman has ten silver coins and loses one. Doesn't she light a lamp, sweep the house and search carefully until she finds it? ⁹ And when she finds it, she calls her friends and neighbours together and says, 'Rejoice with me; I have found my lost coin.' ¹⁰ In the same way, I tell you, there is rejoicing in the presence of the angels of God over one sinner who repents."

When we hear this story, one of the questions we usually ask ourselves is this: Why was she looking for one lost coin when she still had nine coins? It doesn't make much sense to us. In many countries, coins are usually worth only a tiny amount. However, in NT times, a coin was equivalent to a whole day's work, and many people lived on what they earned for the day. While this makes a big difference, the distinctions don't end here.

Ten silver coins were the dowry given to enable a woman to marry. Women would gather these coins in a diadem that hung on their foreheads – something like a ring today. Since diadems symbolized love and commitment, it was unthinkable to lose even a single coin.

Therefore, this woman lights a lamp and cleans the house so she could find the coin. Although this may sound like a simple task, in first-century Palestine, houses had stone floors with large cavities and gaps, and the lighting was poor because the houses had few windows so that they would stay cool in summer and warm in winter. Finding a small coin on a cracked floor in a dimly lit house was almost impossible.

Therefore, when she finds what she has been looking for so desperately, the woman calls her friends and neighbours to celebrate. She has found that symbol of the pact of love that she made with her partner. Now, I invite you to see how, deep down, this familiar story holds transformational power.

Window: Invitation

At the end of the parable, Jesus says, "In the same way, I tell you, there is rejoicing in the presence of the angels of God over one sinner who repents" (15:10). Jesus is comparing the actions of God, Creator of heaven and earth, with the actions of a woman. Can you imagine how subversive this was in the patriarchal and macho society in which he lived?

At the same time, this parable reveals to us a God who is committed and willing to do anything to find the lost. However, this is not a mere metaphor. As one of the most memorized verses in the Bible says, "For God so loved the world that he gave his one and only Son, that whoever believes in him shall not perish but have eternal life" (John 3:16). This is not simple poetry or a figurative image. God became man, lived with the poor, was rejected and marginalized, and died on a cross – the most painful and humiliating death of the time – in order to rescue all humanity.

Recall what we considered earlier – about the efforts you might have made to find something valuable that you had lost. How much more will God do to find his children, whom he has created in his image and likeness? What God did to find the lost is beyond our imagination, and that is why the joy and celebration in heaven is so great over just one person who changes their life.

Mirror: Intimidation

Therefore, if you did not know about God's love and his sacrifice for you, or if you walked away from him or failed to walk in his ways, he has already done everything to reconnect with you. No love or sacrifice is more significant than his, and you are invited to repent and accept it. Then, through communion with him and the embodiment of his message, you can become part of his community and part of the celebration in heaven and earth over the restoration of the relationship between God and his creation.

On the other hand, if you feel superior to others – judging their lives or the lives of those they seek to reach – you might be more like the Pharisees than you would like to be. Ask that God's compassion and his reconciling Spirit fill you. May the way God sees the lost change your perspective and make your heart beat with the same passion that Christ has for them.

Door: Incarnation

Just like the woman in the story, who did everything in her power to find the lost coin, we must open the door, come out of the walls of our temples, and do everything in our power to reach and share God's love with people who have been rejected and marginalized by society and, sadly, even the church. Even though our race, origin, culture, ideology, values, or actions may be different from theirs, we are not exempt from showing them the love of our Father.

As followers of Jesus, we are called to imitate him. It is not enough to share his message. We need to embody it. We must live his message in every interaction with our family, church, work, and society. Only in this way will we be recognized by others as children of God and as agents of peace, justice, and reconciliation in this world full of war, inequality, and transgression. In this way, we can be part of the celebration and joy of God's community.

Observation and Discussion

Esteban does a number of different things in this sermon. Let's focus on them as we expand and deepen the discussion on the model being used.

1. Before he paints a Picture of the parable, Esteban wants his listeners to feel the emotion of panic. The sermon starts in the world of the contemporary listener, not in the world of Jesus. What do you think are the advantages of adopting this approach?

2. Another feature of this sermon is the delayed reading of the Bible passage, with "Information" being shared on either side of that reading. What do you think are the advantages and disadvantages of this delay?

3. Another difference in this sermon is that the order of Mirror and Window are reversed, resulting in "Invitation" coming before "Intimidation." Why do you think Esteban makes this change? What

is the advantage of considering the God of the "how much more" before considering ourselves?

4. The final section is marked by "Incarnation" and how "we must open the door"; but Esteban also adds another phrase – "come out of the walls of our temples." How does that impact our response to this parable?

5. With this sermon, Esteban reminds us that it is important not to be too rigid or legalistic when using this model. Let's remain engaged with our creativity and try different things in the service of the gospel.

14

The Persistent Widow (Luke 18:1–8)

Wilfredo Weigandt

Creating the Sermon Using the Picture-Mirror-Window-Door Model

After carefully studying Luke 18:1–8, bearing in mind the skills for interpreting the parables that were discussed in chapter 2, the sermon structure can be created. In the chart (Figure 21), the descriptions that best show the parable moving through the stages of Picture-Mirror-Window-Door are selected. The choices made for this sermon are shown below:

When preaching a parable, look . . .			
at the Picture	*in* the Mirror	*through* the Window	*beyond* the Door
We see life	We see ourselves	We see God	We see others
Sight	Insight	Vision	Imagination
Information	Intimidation	Invitation	Incarnation
Somebody else	Me!	God and me	God, me, and others
I'm interested	I'm shattered	I'm challenged	I'm called
Knowledge	Conviction	Revelation	Response

(Figure 21)

The Sermon
Luke 18:1–8

> Then Jesus told his disciples a parable to show them that they should always pray and not give up. ² He said, "In a certain town there was a judge who neither feared God nor cared what people thought. ³ And there was a widow in that town who kept coming to him with the plea, 'Grant me justice against my adversary.'
>
> ⁴ "For some time he refused. But finally he said to himself, 'Even though I don't fear God or care what people think, ⁵ yet because this widow keeps bothering me, I will see that she gets justice, so that she won't eventually come and attack me!'"
>
> ⁶ And the Lord said, "Listen to what the unjust judge says. ⁷ And will not God bring about justice for his chosen ones, who cry out to him day and night? Will he keep putting them off? ⁸ I tell you, he will see that they get justice, and quickly. However, when the Son of Man comes, will he find faith on the earth?"

As a disciple of Jesus, have you experienced situations of personal injustice? Who has not! Think about instances where you were treated unjustly by a boss, a co-worker, a close relative, a neighbour, a seller, a buyer, a sister from the church, a pastor, or the municipal, provincial, or national state. Did you cry out in faith? Some of those times of crying out in faith might have been short-lived, whereas others lasted much longer. These everyday realities are challenging! It is worth looking at such situations in the light of the parable recorded in Luke 18:1–8.

Luke's is an expansive and challenging gospel that opens up the good news of salvation through Christ to marginalized groups: Gentiles, the sick, women, tax collectors, Samaritans, children, poor, oppressed, sinners. This emphasis presents Jesus as a teacher capable of confronting the religiosity that had been established in first-century Palestine, an issue that he often challenged through his parables.

In Luke 18:1–14, Luke records two parables that show his intention to deal with issues impacting the Christian communities with which he was linked. The first parable (18:1–8) presents the theme of persevering prayer and the faith necessary to approach a just God who responds to his children who face injustice. The second parable (18:9–14) presents the issue of approaching God with presumed righteousness based on observance of the law (as seen in the Pharisee) rather than with humility (as seen in the tax collector).

Picture: Information

- The parable before us (18:1–8) must be viewed in the light of Jesus's intention in telling it, which was to teach his disciples about the need to persist in prayer, without getting discouraged or giving up. We begin with a picture (18:2–5), in which we see a true-to-life story containing elements that would have been common and credible in first-century Palestine.
- an inconsiderate judge, who is incapable of realizing his wickedness even when he is in the presence of a person before whom he should be ashamed because of his attitude.
- a widow who insistently asks that her case be heard but does not have either a male protector who can pressure the judge or money to bribe the judge.
- an adversary of the widow.
- a court case where the judge protects the adversary. Perhaps the adversary is an influential person or has already bribed the judge.
- a judge who is upset and frustrated because he realizes that the widow will not give up and is going to make his life miserable.

This is the picture; it opens the imagination . . .

At this bend in the road to Jerusalem, under the olive groves that provide shade for us – where the sun and the Samaritan heat don't seem so bothersome – we listen to Jesus's story.

Thomas nods his head. John smiles because he also understands the parable that Jesus tells. The look on Andrew's face indicates that he, too, is impacted by this parable.

Is this story for everyone? This story is common and credible. We can imagine it with our eyes closed, and we are able to relate mentally to each of the places, characters, and situations in the narrative.

Mirror: Intimidation

Then we have a mirror: "And the Lord said, 'Listen to what the unjust judge says'" (18:6). This unexpected reference to the unjust judge is surprising, both because of its absurdity and its unpleasantness. The disciples are expected to consider the unjust judge and learn from him.

> *"What?!" James stammers, almost in horror.*
>
> *Peter can't bear the provocation. He stands up. His insides feel upset as he absorbs the impact of Jesus's words.*
>
> *Bartholomew's dishevelled face asks for an explanation.*
>
> *"No! He cannot be a Teacher!" argues Peter. "How is there anything to learn from an unjust judge?"*
>
> *"How should we – your disciples, people of the kingdom, who practice different and better behaviours – take into account the sayings of this deplorable being? We definitely can't consider his example!"*
>
> *"What is this, Master?"*

What Jesus shows in the mirror intimidates and provokes.

Sectarian ethics was not just the heritage of Jewish religiosity in first-century Palestine. The disciples had also incorporated these attitudes and were prisoners of it. Centuries of hearing such ideas from the mouths of their teachers, centuries of thinking like them, centuries of living according to such beliefs, centuries of tradition . . . all these, Jesus now mercilessly shakes.

Jesus's words reveal the reality that the disciples cannot perceive his message with their eyes and heart. It's a lot to take in for them. But they love this Teacher, who affirms his teachings of life while advancing determinedly towards Jerusalem. Although they struggle internally, they accept the challenge presented to them as they look in the mirror.

Window: Invitation

We find ourselves looking through the window of this parable (18:7–8). God is the central character, dominating the landscape seen through this window. Jesus uses questions to proclaim the reasoning that follows, which makes the decision even more challenging for the confronted disciples. Not only are they forced to rethink from whom they can learn to be good disciples of Jesus, now they must reconsider the God to whom they pray, his character, and his actions. Do you believe that God will bring justice to his children who cry out to him? Do you think that God will listen to you and answer you soon?

> *Jesus's questions challenge us profoundly. We almost feel hurt by them. We realize that our experience of God is at stake in our answer: Who is God really for us, the praying ones?*
>
> *The silence becomes unbearable, so Judas decides to take a few steps around the olive tree that protects him from the oppressive Samaritan noonday sun.*
>
> *"And what do we answer now?" he comments in Matthew's ear. "This path is so difficult and demanding!"*
>
> *"We feel that Jesus, with his questions, is inviting us to look at God."*

The disciples' gaze is directed towards the imaginary window. There they discover that God is real. Jesus himself responds forcefully: "And will not God bring about justice for his chosen ones, who cry out to him day and night?" (18:7).

> *We experience Jesus's intervention as both a relief and an invitation. His gaze and his words heal us.*

Door: Incarnation

Finally, towards the end of verse 8, we have a door.

The disciples are called to imagine and incarnate. Jesus has issued a challenge and the decision is urgent. When the Son of Man returns, will he find conviction, action, and faith in his disciples?

> *Thomas puts his hands to his head and throws a question to the group: "Is this what we want for our lives?"*
>
> *And, almost begging Jesus to say "no," he looks at the calm face of Jesus: "So much is demanded of us, Master!"*
>
> *There is absolute silence. Jesus looks at him and looks at us with love.*
>
> *His lesson through the parable has been masterful: simple, provocative, experiential, direct, accessible, mobilizing.*
>
> *Jesus has challenged our preconceptions and called us to change, to go through that door and venture to apply what was discovered.*
>
> *Nobody dares to look up. Questions pierce our hearts:*
>
> *Will I be able to have the faith that leads me to pray constantly, and without discouragement, for the Lord's intervention on behalf of my fellow believers when God seems distant and elusive?*
>
> *Will I be able to believe – against all evidence – that God is a just judge, who listens to his children in situations of vulnerability?*
>
> *"Come on, my friends! Cheer up!" The voice of Jesus pulls us out of our sorrow.*
>
> *"There are answers on the road ahead to Jerusalem!"*

Let us walk through the door that Jesus opens through the telling of this parable. Let us pray persistently, believing in a just God who responds to the injustices experienced by his children. What impact would this parable have had in the context of the hearers or readers of the Gospel of Luke? This parable must have encouraged believers in the early church to pray without giving up – knowing that God works in history – and to seek God with renewed faith even when he seemed elusive and this filled them with mistrust.

Do we feel God is a just God in the face of the injustices that afflict us? And when injustices are prolonged – what about our faith in him then? Are our beliefs about the very character of God at stake in such moments? In my case, the answer is "yes." How about in yours? God's justice does not imply that his children do not suffer or will not be victims of injustice. Rather, in such times, God intends that we not give up on the God we know and trust.

At the conclusion of the parable, Jesus himself affirmed that God is a just God. Our prayer must be based on this certainty of God's justice.

Let us walk through the door that Jesus opens through the telling of this parable. Let us pray persistently, believing in a just God who responds to the injustices suffered by his children.

We may sometimes see God's action immediately, right before our eyes.

But other times, we may have to wait our whole life before God's actions become evident.

And at times, we may never see God's actions, although others may see it in the distant future.

All this depends on the plans of the God who calls us to hold on in faith while we pray.

The Jesus of this parable calls us to renew our vision and to recreate theology and life transformed by persevering prayer that believes in a just God who responds to his children in the face of the injustices they experience. Amen!

Observation and Discussion

As with the previous sermon from Esteban in chapter 13, Wilfredo plays with our model and helps us see new ways in which it can be utilized.

1. A key feature of this sermon is the way Wilfredo shifts, repeatedly and suddenly, into narrative mode. He imagines the conversation among the disciples as the parable progresses. What is he looking to achieve by adopting this approach?

2. Notice how Wilfredo begins the Picture section with questions for his listeners before placing the parable in its immediate context, and giving insights from Luke's wider agenda. Then he comes to the "true-to-life story containing elements that would have been common and credible in first-century Palestine" about a widow. How does the "Information" he reveals open up each of these features?

3. Once again, the Mirror section is about recovering the shock in the parable: listening to an unjust judge and learning from him! The imaginary dialogue between the disciples expresses their emotional reactions. How does this work to speak to us and for us, drawing us into the experience of "Intimidation"?

4. Wilfredo captures something of the purpose of all the parables when he asserts that the "Invitation" in this one is to "rethink" God – gaining a fresh vision of him through the Window. What is that vision and how does an unlikely character – an "unjust judge" – contribute to it?

5. In the "Incarnation," the parable is referred to as "simple, provocative, experiential, direct, accessible, mobilizing." Reflect on each of these descriptions. How is each one a feature of this sermon? How do these features work together to press us "through the door that Jesus opens" and into a life of persistence in prayer?

15

The Pharisee and the Tax Collector (Luke 18:9–14)

Wilfredo Weigandt

Creating the Sermon Using the Picture-Mirror-Window-Door Model

After carefully studying Luke 18:9–14, bearing in mind the skills for interpreting the parables discussed in chapter 2, the sermon structure can be created. In the chart (Figure 22), the descriptions that best show the parable moving through the stages of Picture-Mirror-Window-Door are selected. The choices made for this sermon are shown below:

When preaching a parable, look . . .			
at the Picture	*in* the Mirror	*through* the Window	*beyond* the Door
We see life	We see ourselves	We see God	We see others
Sight	Insight	Vision	Imagination
Information	Intimidation	Invitation	Incarnation
Somebody else	Me!	God and me	God, me, and others
I'm interested	I'm shattered	I'm challenged	I'm called
Knowledge	Conviction	Revelation	Response

(Figure 22)

The Sermon
Picture: We See Life

We went as a group to meet him.

Two travellers who had entered our village earlier commented on the presence of Jesus and his disciples on the road leading to Jerusalem, so we decided to go out to see them.

From a distance, they must have already seen us – the colour and elegance of our clothes, our bearing, and the ceremonial way in which we walk distinguishes us from the others. We soon found out that Zadkiel – the undesirable tax collector of the village – was also advancing on Jesus. We stopped immediately so as not to get too close to him. We were afraid that his clothing might touch us and make us ceremonially unclean.

When we were just a few metres away from Jesus and his disciples, we saw how the tax collector approached him without observing the minimum distance required of sinners. Jesus didn't seem bothered. This immediately indicated to us his inability as a rabbi to place this despicable man at a distance fitting for one who collected taxes for Rome.

"Bad start," said Sofer, who was one of the brightest stars in our group. We nodded, concerned. Jesus greeted Zadkiel, and then we heard the tax collector babbling out of place – he was actually begging God for mercy for his depravity! In disbelief and outrage, our chief Netaniel dropped to his knees on the ground and exclaimed loudly, "Blasphemy! Yahweh Adonai is not contaminated with the iniquity of tax collectors! Death before mercy for a sinner! Blasphemy!"

Tense silence settled over the scene.

Jesus searched our eyes. We did not hide the unpleasant surprise that filled our eyes or the anger that consumed us inside. Very sure of himself, Baruch – a consecrated member of our Pharisaic sect – pointed to Zadkiel and asked: "Mercy?"

The knowing gaze between our group had given rise to small uncontrollable smiles, which transformed into mocking and expansive laughter at such a ridiculous and reprehensible request. Out of nowhere, with a powerful voice, Jesus interrupted our laughter with his words "Two men went up to the temple to pray . . ." (18:10).

It took a few seconds for us to realize that this pretend prophet had started a story. In front of everyone, he unfolded a picture, perfectly placed. His story contained familiar information – the temple in Jerusalem and the time of public prayer there, either at nine in the morning or three in the afternoon.

"Two men went up to the temple to pray," he repeated, this time calmly and deliberately. And then the unexpected happened.

In a gesture of affection, the Nazarene took Zadkiel's arm – which generated a shout from one of our group, Yosef: "Pollution! Distance! Intolerable dirt!"

Ignoring the uproar, Jesus asked for silence and repeated, forcefully this time, "Two men went up to the temple to pray." Then he began to walk towards us, bringing the sinner with him. As he advanced, the tension became increasingly unbearable. His gaze burned into us.

Glancing first at Yosef and then at our entire group, Jesus continued, "one a Pharisee and the other a tax collector" (18:10).

Mirror: Me!

We immediately perceived that our prominent theological faction of Judaism was one of the main characters in this story. We were there. History was the mirror for us.

Us!

His story was about us – we who cultivate a just and correct interpretation of the Torah, and teach that God's mercy is applicable not to sinners but to those who observe the law. That we believe in the goodness of merits before a holy God.

The other character in the story? One who should not even be named. A traitor of our brothers and our people – accustomed to taking advantage of his "official" position and enjoying the protection of the Roman Empire. A thief – a disgraced person in the eyes of the Lord.

Jesus continued with the story: "The Pharisee stood by himself and prayed: 'God, I thank you that I am not like other people – robbers, evildoers, adulterers – or even like this tax collector. I fast twice a week and give a tenth of all I get" (18:11-12).

As the story unravelled, the tension seemed to ease. We felt that the parable might even come in handy! The grim features of my companions were beginning to relax. Jesus accurately and properly described our referential and preferential place within the town, above other unworthy beings such as thieves, criminals, adulterers, tax collectors – and I assure you the list could go on. His story made clear our zeal for the God of Israel, our most successful activities, our inner holiness, our honourable attitudes.

He spoke of fasting, a strong discipline in our life! An external observance that bears witness to our piety, an activity that we practise – even beyond what Yahweh asks of his people – by fasting every Monday and Thursday.

He spoke of the tithe, another rule that is ingrained in our lives, which manifests this radical attitude that we cultivate as pious leaders of Israel, tithing not only on whatever we earn but also on whatever we sell.

"But the tax collector stood at a distance. He would not even look up to heaven, but beat his breast and said, 'God, have mercy on me, a sinner" (18:13).

This part of the story was like a mirror, where each of us could see ourselves portrayed. Each character in the parable was in the place corresponding to their station in life, and their actions showed the typical dignity or unworthiness of each. That was good! The physical, social, and religious distance maintained between the characters in the parable seemed like a rule plucked out of our manual of righteousness and merit.

The picture that transformed into a mirror was moving in the right direction – it was up to this tax collector for Rome to keep his distance! He did not deserve to even look up to heaven! It was right that he beat his chest! He deserved to lay hold of Yahweh's compassion and immediately be rejected! Nothing about him made him worthy of a place like ours, a place of constant closeness to God!

We were more excited now, as we listened to Jesus. He seemed to understand the ritual codes and the true manifestations of Jewish piety. Even he himself already seemed more like one of us! Every day, we sit in the House of Understanding to dedicate ourselves more deeply to God and get farther away from sinners. At last, Jesus was on our side! He had to take our side some day and that day was today! The tax collector's condemnation felt certain.

Everything was heading in that direction . . .

This mirror showed reality as it is. This mirror showed "Me!"

Window: We See God

And again, the unexpected happened: the picture that had transformed into a mirror now opened a window – a window revealing God. But I must confess, Jesus appeared to be a killjoy! "I tell you that this man [the tax collector], rather than the other [the Pharisee], went home justified before God" (18:14).

After our indignant murmurs died down, silence paralyzed the scene. Then, unexpectedly, Jesus came

towards me: "What do you think about this?" he challenged me. "Something to say?"

As I looked around at my companions, I was embarrassed. My thoughts collided, tearing each other apart. An internal debate raged in my mind: How can God be pleased with a sinner and not with us? It is an impossibility, a contradiction of our understanding and experience of piety in Israel. What kind of God can forgive and approve of a tax collector and leave an honourable Pharisee empty-handed? This can only happen in a story conceived by an impostor like Jesus, someone unable to perceive and value the spirituality that our institution has been cultivating for centuries as God's people. All our lives, we have tried to be pleasing to the Lord, with painstaking, demanding, sacrificial, committed, and relentless zeal! And this impersonator of a rabbi wants to subvert everything.

"Do you think that you, Sanén, deserve to return home justified and Zadkiel does not?" Jesus asked. "Do you believe that God's mercy is for the righteous and not for sinners? Are these so-called righteous ones really righteous?" he continued insistently. "Or are they also sinners just like this tax collector?!"

Faced with these questions, we erupted in loud protests.

My companions surrounded me, yelling at him. But the Nazarene did not flinch. Turning to me again, he continued, "You who consider yourself a pious Jew because of your meticulous observance of the law, do you think that Zadkiel's humility is despicable to God? What if I tell you that you are despicable before God because of the satisfaction and pride that you have in your own justice?"

Hearing this, my colleagues hurled new insults at him.

But my silence became even more deafening. I could hardly think straight.

Where does Jesus get this perspective of God? I never imagined that this window would introduce us to such a God. We don't know God in this way! As a Pharisee, I find this Jesus inconceivable! He is calling into question all my values and behaviours! The force of his declarations ripped through me. I felt that God was inquiring about me, about our school of thought, and about the rest of those people whom we despised.

The tumult slowly faded.

Once things had calmed down, Jesus looked tenderly at Zadkiel and hugged him.

It was too much for me. I did not know, nor could I respond to the surprise that settled first on the face and then on the whole body of the tax collector. We were all stunned at this embrace, which was out of place, polluting, and immodest. The tax collector's shouts of thanks pierced my ears; his joyous dance was both disorderly and embarrassing. Worst of all, Jesus was also happy with him. With his humanity, Jesus embraced all the vileness of Zadkiel, the impostor looked at us and said, "For all those who exalt themselves will be humbled, and those who humble themselves will be exalted" (18:14). I felt the tremendous challenge of this parable from the mouth of the Nazarene.

Door: I'm Called

It was like a door opening after a gruelling battle with God himself. A radical and furious call to review life, a major challenge to unlearn what I thought I knew and to relearn what, for this presumed Messiah, is the true religion of Israel. I was confronted with a new understanding of what it meant to trust in the mercy and forgiveness of Yahweh, not in our own merits, since – according to him – there are none. I was forced to rethink what I perceived as unfair and – according to Jesus's proposal – urgently discard my presumed righteousness and not give rise to self-exaltation. I was challenged to not despise the simplicity of anyone and embrace – according to Jesus's vision – humility as a way of approaching God.

What appeared to be a promising tale turned out to be a barrage of stinging challenges.

"To some who were confident of their own righteousness and looked down on everyone else, Jesus told this parable" (18:9).

One by one, we started on our way home.

A shocking idea assailed me: How should I – recognized by the people as a worthy Pharisee but unknown and unworthy of the Nazarene – connect with God according to this door that Jesus had opened with his parable?

Could it be that presumed righteousness obstructs Yahweh's forgiveness while humility makes it possible?

Could it be that this prophet without institutional credentials can really bring me closer to the Lord?

And what about you? You who are observing my struggle as my story unfolded. Do you think you are immune from its message? I will leave you to wrestle with your own questions in your own day and age . . .

How did this parable resonate down the ages, in the differing contexts of the various hearers or readers of the Gospel of Luke? Could it have been applicable in times when sinners, people of ill-repute, and social outcasts turned to God with nothing but a humble disposition?

Could it have been relevant in times when Gentiles and women were seeking to join Christian churches which were dominated by civil servants of the Roman Empire, pious Jews, and rich people who belonged to the aristocracy?

Could it have been inspiring in times when thieves, criminals, and adulterers sought God's forgiveness and wanted to join the churches where Christians gathered in homes?

Could it be that through this outrageous parable "I'm called"?

Jesus, his disciples, the apostles, and the early church made it clear that justification is a gift from God, a gift that is neither earned nor merited, a gift that requires humility and is received only through Jesus Christ.

What resonated with you as this parable unfolded before you?
How does the God in this parable relate to the God whom you know?
What does the God of this parable call you to change?
Let me share some issues which the parable confronts me about.

- The call to get closer to God from my reality rather than based on self-confidence in "evangelical merits." Evangelicals are, theoretically, heirs of "grace alone . . . faith alone" and oppose the idea of "justification by works." But many times, in our life of faith, we take pride in a long list of merits or an alleged righteousness that differentiates us from others.
- The call to approach the Lord with humility, without allowing the "little evangelical Pharisee that we carry within" to hold others in contempt. The self-esteem that leads to contempt for others is a serious affront to other Christians, and an attitude that distances us from God and his kingdom.
- The call to draw closer to God through an encounter with Jesus Christ and receive justification by the compassionate grace of God in Christ. Encountering the work of Christ brings us closer to God. It also humanizes us and makes us look at ourselves as we really are – whether as those who are far away from God; whether people of ill-repute or those who are socially recognized, far away from God; and yet, seeing that we are accepted when we see ourselves through the eyes of Jesus.

The encounter with Jesus Christ through the door that this parable opens clarifies reality for us and calls us to humility so that the grace that God shows

in Christ reaches and heals us. May it be so in us and in the church of Jesus Christ, through the Holy Spirit, for the glory of God the Father.
Amen.

Observation and Discussion

The model presented in this sermon is like the scaffolding of a building – it is there to help us create the sermon but does not need to be seen in the completed sermon. Reflecting on what Wilfredo does with this sermon can help us to be creative in the way we apply the model.

1. Once again, Wilfredo is doing different things. How would you describe the features of these differences when compared with the earlier sermons? What are the advantages of preaching a parable in this way?

2. In "We see life," notice how Wilfredo explains crucial details relating to the historical background as he retells the story. Furthermore, this retelling of the parable-story is dispersed throughout the sermon. Notice how this works to slow the listener down, creating space for different responses to emerge as the parable unfolds.

3. The challenge with this parable is that we are too familiar with it. After two thousand years, we know that the Pharisee is the bad person and the tax collector is the good person. In Jesus's time, however, the reverse was the reality. So, for us, the shock is gone. It must be recovered if the "Me!" section is to register any impact. What does Wilfredo do to help us feel the shock again?

4. In the section explaining the Window (Chapter 6), we learned of the importance of preacher and listeners becoming "as one of the characters." In "We see God," how does retelling the story and naming the characters help this to happen?

5. With "I'm called," Wilfredo utilizes questions and testimony, two features of effective preaching. With the latter, notice how we hear someone else being challenged – first the "they" (the characters in the sermon) and then the "him" (the preacher – Wilfredo) – before we ourselves – the "me" (the listener or reader) – are challenged.

Epilogue

Wilfredo Weigandt

We see this book as part of the multifaceted grace of God that enriches interculturality.

We who write this live in different parts of the world and represent different cultures; we express our faith in Christ in different ways and cultivate it in different denominational spaces; and we belong to a community of preachers that promotes expository preaching and the training of preachers in different cultures and nations.

The parable genre was conceived and developed centuries ago, in geographies and cultures different from those that we experience today as writers. Our venture into the study and biblical preaching of Jesus's parables has taken us to a new level of interculturality.

Our preaching of the parables that we have shared here took place in specific cultural settings. The application and content in the sermons in this book dialogue with and respond to the challenges and opportunities in the cultures of each one of us in our role as biblical expositors.

We share culturally open material, and we want it to open again in the context of each reader. This implies an essential exercise in intercultural hermeneutics, where the colour of each lens will open the world and faith in each reading.

We perceive that these various expressions of interculturality occur within a framework of respect for and celebration of diversity and one's own cultural identity, which are God's gifts. When well conducted, such expressions of interculturality may generate a more vibrant faith and a healthy synergy between the various expressions of preaching ministries in the world.

The interculturality present in the parables exposes us to multiple dimensions of approaches, meanings, and applications.

Some parables link us to the *individual dimension* of our Christian spirituality. Who is "my neighbour" (Luke 10:29–37) today in a globalized world? What consequences flow from the call to me as a believer to be a "wise" person rather than a "foolish" person (Matt 7:24–27) in the light of Jesus's words about life's foundations? How do I "pray and not give up" (Luke 18:2–8) when facing injustice and suffering?

Some parables link us to the *community dimension* of our faith in Jesus.

What does it mean to be the owner of a house who brings out of his or her "storeroom new treasures as well as old" (Matt 13:52) in teaching and preaching the Scriptures in our churches? What attitude does the Christian community have towards "the lost sheep" (Luke 15:4–7)? What attitudes must we cultivate before the return of Jesus Christ if we are to be a church inspired by the five wise virgins (Matt 25:1–13)?

Some parables link us to the *social dimension* of our countries and cultures.

What does it mean today to be "salt" and "light" (Matt 5:13–16) in a world of decay and shadow? What is expected of a judge in our society in light of God who is a just judge (Luke 18:2–8)? What is the link between "the wheat" and "the weeds" (Matt 13:24–30, 36–43) with reference to the growth of God's kingdom and the kingdom of the evil one in society today?

Some parables link us to the *environmental dimension* of our universe.

How does our "gardener" Father's care for the vine (John 15:1–6) inspire our care for his creation? In what way is the generosity and abundant life of "the sower" (Matt 13:3–8, 18–23) an example for our sowing towards the totality of creation?

The preaching of parables – which interweaves these dimensions of interculturality in a healthy manner – empowers us with the faith to integrate these vital spaces under the guidance of the Spirit of God.

Preaching parables in this era will put us in contact with elements of faith to live the environmental aspects of our Christian life in a manner that honours our Creator God.

Preaching parables to humanity today will lead us to both affirm and challenge the culture and life of our peoples and nations, and to integrate this social dimension into our Christian discipleship.

Preaching parables in our churches today will make us wonder about the growth of the community of Jesus Christ in the here and now of our cultures.

Preaching parables at this time will prompt us to address central issues of our personal faith and to open ourselves to the work of the Holy Spirit in our individual lives.

We – who have dreamed and worked on this book – now release this work to the cultures of the world so that they may experience parable-inspired interculturality guided by the Creator of all culture. We pray that the kingdom of God and his justice will grow from this initiative.

Amen.

Bibliography

Bailey, Kenneth E. *Poet and Peasant, and Through Peasant Eyes: A Literary-Cultural Approach to the Parables in Luke*. Grand Rapids: Eerdmans, 1976.

Blomberg, Craig L. *Interpreting the Parables*. 2nd ed. Downers Grove: IVP Academic, 2012.

Bock, Darrell L. *Luke 1:1–9:50*. BECNT. Grand Rapids: Baker Academic, 1994.

Bowling, John C. *Windows and Mirrors: Exploring the Parables of Jesus*. Kansas City: Foundry, 2020.

Brueggemann, Walter. *First and Second Samuel: A Bible Commentary for Preaching and Teaching*. Louisville: John Knox Press, 1990.

———. *Spirituality of the Psalms*. Minneapolis: Fortress Press, 2002.

Clements, Roy. *A Sting in the Tale*. Leicester: IVP, 1995.

Crossan, John Dominic. "The Good Samaritan: Towards a Generic Definition of Parable." *Semeia* 2 (1974): 82–112.

Dodd, C. H. *The Parables of the Kingdom*. London: Nisbet, 1935.

Donahue, John R. *The Gospel in Parable: Metaphor, Narrative, and Theology in the Synoptic Gospels*. Philadelphia: Fortress Press, 1988.

Duke, Paul Simpson. *The Parables: A Preaching Commentary*. Nashville: Abingdon, 2005.

Fleming, David L. *What is Ignatian Spirituality?* Chicago: Loyola Press, 2008.

Green, Joel B. *The Gospel of Luke*. NICNT. Grand Rapids: Eerdmans, 1997.

Herzog, William R, II. *Parables as Subversive Speech: Jesus as Pedagogue of the Oppressed*. Louisville: Westminster John Knox, 1994.

Hughes, Robert G. "Preaching the Parables." In *The Promise and Practice of Biblical Theology*, edited by John Henry Paul Reumann, 157–70. Minneapolis: Fortress Press, 1991.

Hultgren, Arland J. *The Parables of Jesus: A Commentary*. Grand Rapids: Eerdmans, 2000.

Hunter, A. M. *The Parables: Then and Now*. London: SCM, 1971.

Jeremias, Joachim. *The Parables of Jesus*. London: SCM, 1963.

Jones, G. V. *The Art and Truth of the Parables*. London: SPCK, 1964.

Keener, Craig S. *A Commentary on the Gospel of Matthew*. Grand Rapids: Eerdmans, 1999.

Klausen, Jytte. *The Cartoons That Shook the World*. New Haven: Yale University Press, 2009.

Kreglinger, Gisela H. *Storied Revelations: Parables, Imagination, and George MacDonald's Christian Fiction*. Eugene: Pickwick, 2013.

Krieger, Murray. *A Window to Criticism: Shakespeare's Sonnets and Modern Poetics*. Princeton: Princeton University Press, 1964.

Kruschwitz, Jonathan A. "2 Samuel 12:1–15: How (Not) to Read a Parable." *Review and Expositor* 109 (Spring 2012): 253–59.

Long, Thomas G. *Preaching and the Literary Forms of the Bible*. Philadelphia: Fortress Press, 1989.

McKenna, Megan. *Parables: The Arrows of God*. Maryknoll: Orbis, 1994.

Meynell, Mark. *What Angels Long to Read: Reading and Preaching the New Testament*. Carlisle: Langham Preaching Resources, 2017.

Morris, Leon. *Luke*. TNTC. Leicester: IVP, 1974/1988.

Nouwen, Henri J. M. *The Return of the Prodigal Son*. New York: Doubleday, 1992.

Peterson, Eugene H. *Leap Over A Wall: Earthy Spirituality for Everyday Christians*. New York: HarperCollins, 1997.

———. *Tell It Slant: A Conversation on the Language of Jesus in His Stories and Prayers*. Grand Rapids: Eerdmans, 2008.

Powell, Mark Allan. *What Do They Hear? Bridging the Gap Between Pulpit and Pew*. Nashville: Abingdon, 2007.

Schweizer, Eduard. *The Good News according to Luke*. Translated by David E. Green. Atlanta: John Knox, 1984.

———. *The Good News according to Matthew*. Translated by David E. Green. Atlanta: John Knox, 1975.

Scott, Bernard Brandon. *Hear Then the Parable: A Commentary on the Parables of Jesus*. Minneapolis: Fortress Press, 1989.

Snodgrass, Klyne R. *Stories with Intent: A Comprehensive Guide to the Parables of Jesus*. 2nd ed. Grand Rapids: Eerdmans, 2018.

Sulivan, Jean. *Morning Light: The Spiritual Journal of Jean Sulivan*. New York: Paulist Press, 1988.

Takatemjen, "Luke." In *South Asia Bible Commentary*, edited by Brian Wintle, 1327–85. Rajasthan: Open Door, 2015.

Tucker, Jeffrey T. *Example Stories: Perspectives on Four Parables in the Gospel of Luke*. JSNT, Supplement Series 162. Sheffield Academic Press, 1998.

Via, Dan O., Jr. *The Parables: Their Literary and Existential Dimension*. Philadelphia: Fortress Press, 1967.

Weigandt, Wilfredo. *Prayer in the Time of a Pandemic*. Carlisle: Langham Preaching Resources, 2021.

Wenham, David. *The Parables of Jesus: Pictures of Revolution*. London: Hodder and Stoughton, 1989.

Wieland, George M. "Cultivating Attentiveness: Formation for Ministry through the Practice of Intercultural Bible Reading," *Colloquium* 53/1 (2021): 98–117.

Wiersbe, Warren. *Preaching and Teaching with Imagination: the Quest for Biblical Ministry*. Grand Rapids: Baker Books, 1994.

Wiesel, Elie. *The Trial of God*. New York: Schocken Books, 1995.

Wintle, Brian. "Matthew" in *South Asia Bible* Commentary, ed. Brian Wintle. Rajasthan: Open Door, 2015.

Woods, John. *God Is in the House: A Fresh Model for Shaping a Sermon.* Carlisle: Langham Preaching Resources, 2022.
Young, Brad H. *Jesus and His Jewish Parables.* New York: Paulist, 1989.
Zimmerman, Ruben. *Puzzling the Parables: Methods and Interpretations.* Minneapolis: Fortress Press, 2015.

Langham Literature and its imprints are a ministry of Langham Partnership.

Langham Partnership is a global fellowship working in pursuit of the vision God entrusted to its founder John Stott –

> *to facilitate the growth of the church in maturity and Christ-likeness through raising the standards of biblical preaching and teaching.*

Our vision is to see churches in the Majority World equipped for mission and growing to maturity in Christ through the ministry of pastors and leaders who believe, teach and live by the word of God.

Our mission is to strengthen the ministry of the word of God through:
- nurturing national movements for biblical preaching
- fostering the creation and distribution of evangelical literature
- enhancing evangelical theological education

especially in countries where churches are under-resourced.

Our ministry

Langham Preaching partners with national leaders to nurture indigenous biblical preaching movements for pastors and lay preachers all around the world. With the support of a team of trainers from many countries, a multi-level programme of seminars provides practical training, and is followed by a programme for training local facilitators. Local preachers' groups and national and regional networks ensure continuity and ongoing development, seeking to build vigorous movements committed to Bible exposition.

Langham Literature provides Majority World preachers, scholars and seminary libraries with evangelical books and electronic resources through publishing and distribution, grants and discounts. The programme also fosters the creation of indigenous evangelical books in many languages, through writer's grants, strengthening local evangelical publishing houses, and investment in major regional literature projects, such as one volume Bible commentaries like *The Africa Bible Commentary* and *The South Asia Bible Commentary*.

Langham Scholars provides financial support for evangelical doctoral students from the Majority World so that, when they return home, they may train pastors and other Christian leaders with sound, biblical and theological teaching. This programme equips those who equip others. Langham Scholars also works in partnership with Majority World seminaries in strengthening evangelical theological education. A growing number of Langham Scholars study in high quality doctoral programmes in the Majority World itself. As well as teaching the next generation of pastors, graduated Langham Scholars exercise significant influence through their writing and leadership.

To learn more about Langham Partnership and the work we do visit **langham.org**